Entering Into God's Rest

Entering Into God's Rest

By Lowell Smith

eBookstand Books
Division of The Magnum Group
Auburn, CA 95604 USA
1728_3

© 2001. All rights reserved.
No part of this publication may be reproduced by
any means without the prior permission of the author.

ISBN 1-58909-114-0

Printed in the Unites States of America

Entering Into God's Rest

Preface

This book has been ten years in the making. It is written explicitly for Christians who believe the Bible is the infallible and inspired word of God, and therefore, follow after Christ. It is for those who believe that Jesus Christ is the only begotten Son of God, and that Jesus died for their sins. It is for those who believe and confess Jesus as their Savior and Lord according to John 3:16 and Romans 10:9 and 10.

The author believes that the Bible is the Word of God written by men as the Holy Spirit inspired them. The Bible is the sole reference for the teachings in this book. No other reference was used.

The author encourages the reader to have the Bible as a ready reference while reading this book, even though all referenced scriptures are included as they are discussed so the reader may see the scriptures used first hand.

Entering Into God's Rest/Lowell Smith

Table of Contents

Preface
Introduction   1
Chapter 1:
Justified By Faith, Not By Works   9
Chapter 2:
Sanctification   17
Chapter 3:
Righteousness   27
Chapter 4:
The Old Testament and the Law;
The New Testament and Sin   35
Chapter 5:
What is Sin?   51
Chapter 6:
Expediency   59
Chapter 7:
Peace   67
Chapter 8:
Glorious Church Without Spot or Wrinkle
"The Body of Christ"   73
Chapter 9:
Entering Into God's Rest   79

Introduction

The Bible abounds with scriptures telling of a wonderful rest God affords to those who follow Him. The best known of these scriptures may be Matthew 11:28,29.

"Come to me, all ye that labor and are heavy laden, and I will give you rest. Take my yoke upon you, and learn of me; for I am meek and lowly in heart: and ye shall find rest unto your souls."

"Rest unto your souls." That is the ultimate goal. It is a wonderful promise of God that all Christians should pursue and ultimately achieve. Rest unto your souls would mean that we are at peace with God, that we have peace and comfort within ourselves and that we would be devoid of the fear and anxiety that is so common in the world today.

The Bible exhorts us to believe in God and to live according to His principles. We are told that if we do, God will bless us with many blessings, not the least of which are His shelter and His provision. It is in God's divine shelter and provision that we find the wonderful rest promised in Matthew 11:28,29. In God's rest we overcome our fears, rid ourselves of anxieties and face the uncertainties of life without trepidation. Without fear and anxiety to wear upon us, the sun seems to shine brighter and every moment of each day becomes a more pleasant experience. That doesn't mean the world becomes a better place. In fact, the Bible says that wickedness upon the earth shall increase as the return of Christ approaches. Neither does it mean that the life of the true Christian believer becomes void of trials and tribulation. It simply means that, within our spirit, we can enjoy the peace and rest of God in the midst of daily living.

Unfortunately, too many Christians who hear this truth and believe it continue to live in fear, never finding the rest that God offers them. They believe in God. They truly love the Lord. They read the Word and believe it. Yet, because of sin, they continue to have doubts about their faith. They wonder if God can love them when they continue to sin. Some entertain thoughts of giving up, even though they would be reluctant to share such thoughts with fellow Christians. This is because they believe that they alone have those thoughts and feelings. The doubt is not limited to those who sit in the pews. It also affects some of those who stand behind the pulpits and before Sunday School classes.

Why is there so much doubt among committed believers? Where is the shortcoming in the teaching? What is needed to convince believers to trust in God, to take Him at His Word and to enter into His rest? A clear explanation of scripture is required to enable us to understand the nature of sin, the difference between obedience and grace, and the relevance of the Old and New Testaments to believers today. With these understandings of scripture, the reader should be able to apply scriptural truth to daily living in a way that will bring God's rest to the believer.

In order to follow Him, we must first believe in Him, and after we believe in Him we must trust Him. Believing in Him makes Him our Savior. Trusting Him makes Him our Lord. We will not follow someone in whom we do not believe and we will not trust someone in whom we do not have confidence. By definition, a Christian is a person who believes in Jesus as Savior and follows his teachings. That's what makes a person a Christian, a follower of Christ. They believe, by faith, that Jesus died for their sins and by confessing in Him, they are forgiven and saved from the penalty of sin. This is the truth of John 3:16 where the scripture says, "Whosoever believeth in Him shall not perish, but have everlasting life." If you believe in your heart that Jesus died to pay the price for your sins and if you confess that belief openly with your mouth, then you are a child of God (saved) according to Romans 10:9,10. But becoming a child of God does not automatically mean that you have fully appropriated His rest. Some would say that it does, but the scripture shows us this is clearly not true, as does practical life. The Bible also warns believers of the consequences of not trusting enough to enter into the rest that God provides. One such passage is:

Hebrews 3:12 to 4:3.
12. Take heed brethren, lest there be in any of you an evil heart of unbelief, in departing from the living God.
13. But exhort one another daily, while it is called today, lest any of you be hardened through the deceitfulness of sin.
14. For we are made partakers of Christ, if we hold the beginning of our confidence steadfast unto the end.
15. While it is said, today if ye will hear his voice, harden not your hearts, as in the provocation.

16. *For some, when they had heard, did provoke: howbeit not all came out of Egypt by Moses.*
17. *But with whom was He grieved forty years? Was it not with them that had sinned, whose carcasses fell in the wilderness?*
18. *And to whom swear He that they should not enter into His rest, but to them that believed not?*
19. *So, we see that they could not enter in because of unbelief.*

4:1. *Let us therefore fear, lest, a promise being left us of entering into His rest, any of you should seem to come short of it.*
4:2. *For unto us was the gospel preached, as well as unto them. But the word preached did not profit them, not being mixed with the faith of them that heard it.*
4:3. *For we which have believed do enter into rest as he said. As I have sworn in my wrath, if they shall enter into my rest: although the works were finished from the foundation of the world.*

It is of utmost importance that we understand the nature of sinning and unbelief that kept the children of God from obtaining the Promise Land, (God's rest), and how their attitude toward God's promise relates to our daily walk with God today. This understanding will enable us to know what God expects of believers today. It will provide the knowledge we need to walk in the Spirit and not in the flesh, and thereby, please God.

Two important points from the scriptures in Hebrews are: 1, there is a rest for God's people, and 2, God's people can miss entering into that rest because of unbelief.

First, we must note that it was God's people that were guilty of the unbelief. They were the "Children of Israel." There should be no doubt that they believed in God. They saw his presence in a variety of manifestations many times over a period of many years. The unbelief in this passage of scripture does not refer to the unsaved, to those who have not yet believed. Let's be very clear on the first point: God's rest is for God's people and the unbelief was a condition of God's people. So what was the nature of their unbelief? The children of Israel believed "in" God. They were convinced He existed, but they didn't "believe" (trust) God. They knew who He was, but they refused to follow Him. This was the nature of the unbelief in the provocation. It was precisely their unbelief that provoked God. They didn't "please" God with their faith in Him; they "provoked" God with their unbelief.

To learn how to enter into God's rest, let's examine what we are told in **Hebrews 4:3,4.** "The word preached must be mixed with faith for it to profit us, and, we who have believed do enter into His rest."

Notice that the emphasis here is on BELIEVING and not on DOING. Another word for believing is faith. Faith must come first. We hear the truth of God, we mix it with our faith, and then we act.

TRUTH + FAITH = GOOD WORKS

The scripture says that the children of Israel heard the word preached (TRUTH), but they did not mix their faith with it and consequently, that unbelief was reflected in their behavior and they sinned.

TRUTH + UNBELIEF = SINFUL WORKS

Why was it so hard for the children of Israel to believe God? They knew God was real. He led them by day as a pillar of smoke and by night as a pillar of fire. They heard his voice thunder off the mountain on more than one occasion, and they saw the radiance on Moses' face and the tablets of stone containing the Ten Commandments. They saw the water from the rock and they ate the manna and quail from heaven. How does the author of Hebrews justify saying they didn't believe?

The author of Hebrews isn't saying they didn't believe in God, he is saying they didn't believe God. They didn't believe His promises to them. THEY WERE AFRAID. They didn't trust God at His word. He had promised them a land flowing with milk and honey, but once they saw the giants there, they didn't believe God could give it into their hands. This idea of a free gift was totally foreign to them. They had been in slavery for four hundred years. They expected to suffer and work hard for things. They couldn't grasp this new idea that God would just give them something for free, a *gift*. They thought God's promise was too simple, too convenient, and too easy. Certainly there had to be more to it. There must have been something that God wasn't telling them. They wouldn't accept the promises of God at face value. That was their unbelief. They wanted to go back to Egypt because they were afraid to go forward. Their unbelief was having more confidence in themselves and their old ways than trusting and moving ahead with the new promises of God.

We can be in danger of the same type of unbelief. We must be careful to hear what God promises, and then to accept those promises by faith. We must hear the word preached and then mix it with our faith. We must trust God.

Belief and faith are more than just internal actions. They must result in some external outcome as well. The reason so many Christians today still live with fear and anxiety is because they have believed internally, but have not manifested that belief in the things that they do. Faith must move us to action. There must be an outcome that manifests itself outwardly. James covers this beautifully.

James 2:14-24
> 14. *What doth it profit, my brethren, though a man say he hath faith, and have not works? Can faith save him?*
> 15. *If a brother or sister be naked, and destitute of daily food,*
> 16. *and one of you say unto them, depart in peace, be ye warmed and filled, notwithstanding ye give them not those things which are needful to the body, what doth it profit?*
> 17. *Even so faith, if it hath not works, is dead, being alone.*
> 18. *Yea, a man may say, Thou hast faith, and I have works: shew me thy faith without thy works, and I will shew thee my faith by my works.*
> 19. *Thou believest that there is one God, thou doest well: the devils also believe and tremble.*
> 20. *But wilt thou know, O vain man, that faith without works is dead.*
> 21. *Was not Abraham our father justified by works, when he had offered Isaac his son upon the altar?*
> 22. *Seest thou how faith wrought with his works, and by works was faith made perfect?*
> 23. *And the scripture was fulfilled which saith, Abraham believed God, and it was imputed unto him for righteousness: and he was called the Friend of God.*
> 24. *Ye see then how that by works a man is justified, and not by faith only.*

It is no secret that many Biblical scholars have had some trouble with these passages from James. Some have dubbed the book of James the "Epistle of Straw" because it seems to be teaching justification by works and not by faith. But if we look at it closely in conjunction with the rest of the Bible's teaching, we see that James was teaching us an important aspect of faith. The truth here is that, if faith doesn't result in some change in our behavior, then we have come short of the mark. This is the same message we read about the Children of Israel in the passage from Hebrews. They fell short of the Promise Land because of their unbelief. They didn't mix their faith with the truth and move forward. The emphasis here is on "moving forward."

God has promised us something very similar to what he had promised the children of Israel that Moses led out of Egypt. He has promised us a free gift, which brings with it a peace and a rest. Christians today have the same opportunity to move into the spiritual "land of milk and honey," the spiritual "promised land." That free gift is deliverance from the curse of sin and death that was placed upon man in Genesis chapter 3. Death here refers to the second death, the final death that is eternal separation from God. But it also promises rest. Rest from what? Rest from the burden of sin in this life. "This corruptible has not yet put on incorruption," Paul writes in 1Corinthians 15:53. "Come to me," God says, "and I will give you REST."

He promised to save us from our sins, which Jesus did when he hung on the cross. His final words were these, "It is finished." Death, hell and the grave were defeated and the precious blood covered our sins once and for all. We accept this by faith or we cannot have that gift. We hear it preached and we mix it with our faith and it moves us to believe that we are saved. It is only by faith that we can know salvation. By faith, we become Christians. By faith, we live our lives differently. By faith, we follow Christ.

Just like the children of Israel, there is something God has promised us. It is a gift He has given us. It is a gift so wonderful that we find it hard to believe at face value. We have a hard time accepting this gift. The gift is our righteousness. Our sins are forgiven, gone forever, as far as the east is from the west the Bible says. The blood of Christ covers them. We are reconciled with God. It is finished. The price is paid in full. This book discusses that truth in great detail. The consequences of our behavior have been accounted for. We are pure in God's sight regardless of our behavior because we are under the blood by faith.

Like the children of Israel, this kind of statement is not one you may be accustomed to hearing and it will be hard for some to believe and even more difficult for some to apply to their lives. This book discusses scriptures showing why this statement is not only true, but why it is *absolutely essential* for us to please God, enter into his rest and be effective as Christians.

Hebrews 4:1 – 11

1. *Let us therefore fear, lest, a promise being left us of entering into his rest, any of you should seem to come short of it.*
2. *For unto us was the gospel preached, as well as unto them: but the word preached did not profit them, not being mixed with faith in them that heard it.*
3. *For we which have believed do enter into rest, as he said, As I have sworn in my wrath, if they shall enter into my rest: although the works were finished from the foundation of the world.*
4. *For he spake in a certain place of the seventh day on this wise, And God did rest the seventh day from all his works.*
5. *And in this place again, If they shall enter into my rest.*
6. *Seeing therefore it remaineth that some must enter therein, and they to whom it was first preached entered not in because of unbelief:*
7. *Again, he limiteth a certain day, saying in David, To day, after so long a time; as it is said, To day if ye will hear his voice, harden not your hearts.*
8. *For if Jesus had given them rest, then would he not afterward have spoken of another day.*
9. *There remaineth therefore a rest to the people of God.*
10. *For he that is entered into his rest, he also hath ceased from his own works, as God did from his.*
11. *Let us labour therefore to enter into that rest, lest any man fall after the same example of unbelief.*

The scriptural truth in Hebrews 4:1 - 11 is so very, very important. It says that there is a seventh day, a day of REST. This also refers to the seventh dispensation of God's relationship with His creation. The fifth dispensation was the Law. That covenant was with the Children of Israel and began under Moses' leadership chosen of God. The sixth dispensation is Grace and is for all who believe. It is the current dispensation. We are no longer under the law; we are under grace. It is in the seventh day that God ceased from His works (verse 4) and it is in this sixth day (of grace) that we are to cease from our own works (verse 10).

Now, as some tend to jump to conclusions, be assured that this doesn't mean that we are to disregard God's commandments and do what we please. That is not what the scripture is saying at all. That is not the kind of behavior we are talking about, as we will clearly see throughout this book. What it is saying is that our works cannot justify us in God's sight. So we shouldn't bother trying to please God or earn God's favor by our works (behavior). In fact, as we will see in the scripture, this is exactly the wrong thing to do.

This idea may require a renewing of our mind as Paul exhorts in

Romans 12:2;
2. *And be not conformed to this world, but be ye transformed by the renewing of your mind that ye may prove what is that good, and acceptable, and perfect will of God.*

God's word exhorts us to "be transformed by the renewing of our mind." The first new thought that we must plant in our renewed mind is this: our works can never please God nor earn favor with Him, for they are as filthy rags. (Isaiah 64:6)

Chapter One

Justified By Faith, Not By Works

Romans 4:1-8; 17-21; 24-25
1. *What shall we then say that Abraham our father, as pertaining to the flesh, hath found?*
2. *For if Abraham were justified by works, he hath something to glory about; but not before God.*
3. *For what saith the scripture? Abraham believed God, and it was counted to him for righteousness.*
4. *Now to him that worketh is the reward not reckoned of grace, but of debt.*
5. *But to him that worketh not, but believeth on him that justifieth the ungodly, his faith is counted for righteousness.*
6. *Even as David also describeth the blessedness of the man, to whom God imputeth righteousness apart from works,*
7. *saying, Blessed are they whose iniquities are forgiven, and whose sins are covered.*
8. *Blessed is the man to whom the Lord will not impute sin.*

17. For the promise, that he should be the heir of the world, was not to Abraham, or to his seed, through the law, but through the righteousness of faith.
18. For if they who are of the law are heirs, faith is made void, and the promise made of no effect.
19. Because the law worketh wrath: for where the law is, there is no transgression.
20. Therefore it is of faith, that it might be by grace; to the end the promise might be sure to all the seed; not to that only which is of the law, but to that also which is of the faith of Abraham; who is the father of us all,
21. (As it is written, I have made thee a father of many nations), before him whom he believed, even God, who giveth life to the dead, and calleth those things which are not as though they were.

24. But for us also, to whom it shall be imputed, if we believe on him that raised Jesus our Lord from the dead;
25. Who was delivered for our offenses, and raised again for our justification.

Romans 5:1-2; 9; 17-19
1. Therefore being justified by faith, we have peace with God through our Lord Jesus Christ:
2. By whom also we have access by faith into this grace in which we stand, and rejoice in hope of the glory of God.

9. Much more then, being now justified by his blood, we shall be saved from wrath through him.

17. For if by one man's offense death reigned by one; much more they who receive abundance of grace and of the gift of righteousness shall reign in life by one, Jesus Christ.
18. Therefore as by the offense of one, judgment came upon all men to condemnation; even so by the righteousness of one, the free gift came upon all men to justification of life.

19. *For as by one man's disobedience many were made sinners, so by the obedience of one shall many be made righteous.*

Justification and sanctification - we hear these terms used quite often in sermons and Sunday School lessons. They are very important terms to us and we need to understand their meanings precisely. This chapter discusses justification and the next covers sanctification.

According to Webster's Dictionary, justify means: *to prove or show to be right; to qualify; to fit exactly.*

Romans 5:1 and 9 tell us that we are justified by faith, by his blood and we shall be saved from wrath. We are *justified*! We are made *right*! We *qualify*, and we *fit exactly*. And all of this is made possible by two things: His blood and our faith. By simply believing in God, we are made perfect. In addition, we are saved from wrath. Being saved from wrath means we are saved from suffering the consequences of our unrighteousness. God has forgiven us and has justified us by the blood of Christ. We can now take comfort in knowing that we will not have to suffer any of the wrath of God for our sinfulness because that suffering has already been performed by Jesus on our behalf. We are justified.

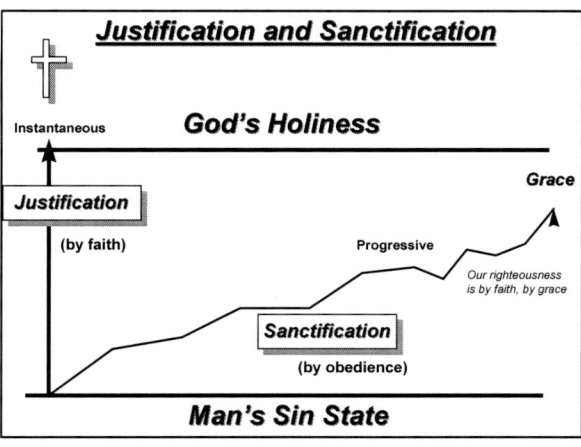

Justification is instantaneous. As this illustration shows, we are justified the moment we believe and accept Jesus as savior and Lord. This is true because Jesus has already done the perfect work necessary for our redemption, and faith is the response that applies it to our life. The only requirement on our part is to believe. God made the sacrifice; we accept His gift to us by faith. Here are the scriptures:

Acts 13:39
39. *And by him **all that believe** are justified from all things, from which ye could not be justified by the Law of Moses.*

Romans 3:28
28. *Therefore we conclude that **a man is justified by faith** apart from the deeds of the law.*

Galatians 2:16
16. *Knowing that **a man is not justified by the works of the law**, but by the faith of Jesus Christ, even we have believed in Jesus Christ, that we may be justified by the faith of Christ, and not by the works of the law: **for by the works of the law shall no flesh be justified.***

Romans 3:20
20. *Therefore by the deeds of the law there shall no flesh be justified in His sight: for by the law is the knowledge of sin.*

Justification does not come by being obedient to the law. That means it does not come by being obedient to the commandments of God. That means it does not come from a righteous and holy lifestyle. That means it is not a product of our behavior. Those things are all associated with sanctification. We are justified only by the precious blood of Jesus Christ and by exercising our faith to accept His perfect and complete work on the cross. There is nothing more that needs to be done. Jesus died for us, we believe that and we are justified. In His own words from the cross, "it is finished."

Romans 4:25
25. *Who (Jesus) was delivered for our offenses and was raised again for our justification.*

Romans 5:18
18. *Therefore as by the offence of one (Adam), judgment came upon all men to condemnation, even so by the righteousness of one (Jesus), the **free gift** came upon all men unto justification of life.*

We cannot improve upon nor can we add to the work that Jesus did on the cross. The redemption of man is **a free gift from God, by grace, imparted through faith.** We must be very careful not to think that we, or any other person, is justified or not justified by behavior. Justification is only by faith in the savior. Look at the account of the two praying in the temple in **Luke 18:10-14.**

10. *Two men went up to the temple to pray; the one a Pharisee, and the other a publican.*
11. *The Pharisee stood and prayed thus with himself, God, I thank thee, that I am not as other men are, extortioners, unjust, adulterers, or even as this publican.*
12. *I fast twice in the week, I give tithes of all that I possess.*
13. *And the publican, standing afar off, would not lift up so much as his eyes unto heaven, but smote upon his breast, saying, God be merciful to me a sinner.*
14. *I tell you, this man went down to his house justified rather than the other: for every one that exalteth himself shall be abased; and he that humbleth himself shall be exalted."*

Jesus himself was the one telling this account and the one speaking the words in verse 14. Like the Pharisee, we err if we try to impress God with our lifestyle or justify our own behavior by comparing ourselves with others. Jesus refers to this as "exalting oneself." And like the Publican, we go away justified when we acknowledge that we are in desperate need of a savior. Jesus refers to this as "humbling oneself." Don't get trapped into this *holier than thou* attitude. That's exactly what the Pharisee did. We cannot save ourselves. Jesus did the perfect and complete work of salvation on the cross and gave that to us as a gift. We need only accept it by faith. Once again, it is obtained by His blood and our faith.

We must always recognize that we cannot gain favor with God through our own works of righteousness (for they are as filthy rags). Favor with God comes only from faith in the Son, by which we obtain grace.

Galatians 5:4
4. *Christ is become of no effect to you, whoever of you are justified by the law; ye have fallen from grace.*

Romans 4:4, 5 and 17b.
4. *Now to him that worketh is the reward not reckoned of grace, but of debt.*
5. *But to him that worketh not, but believeth on him that justified the ungodly, his faith is counted as righteousness."*
17. *even God, who quickeneth the dead, and calleth those things which be not as though they were.*

So why is this understanding so important? What positive affect will it have in me as a Christian? It is only when we fully comprehend that God loves us and sheds his grace upon us based **solely** on the fact that **we believe**, that we can begin to experience the **rest** that God promises to us. We have peace with God knowing he loves and accepts us. Let's examine verses 4 and 5 above. If we work for our salvation, our reward is not of grace but of debt. What is grace? It is "unmerited favor." Unmerited means that we didn't earn it nor do we deserve it. God chooses to shed His grace. Upon whom does he shed His grace? Verse 5 tells us it is upon those who believe on Him that justifies the ungodly. God justifies us while we are yet "ungodly." Our faith, the verse tells us, is counted as our being righteous. Then, verse 17 gives us the conclusion of the truth, and I'll paraphrase: God who is able to bring the dead back alive also has the power to call things something that they are not. In this case, He calls the ungodly people righteous simply because they believe.

The difficulty isn't with God's ability or willingness to justify and accept; the difficulty is in the inability or unwillingness of the believer to accept what God has done. This is the same kind of "unbelief" that the children of Israel had that provoked God and kept them from entering into the Promised Land. If God deems us justified, and he does by His word, then we ought to be able to believe we are justified. If He calls us righteous even while we are still ungodly, shouldn't we be able to accept that for ourselves even though the sin nature still rules in us?

The belief that we are justified must firmly enter into our thoughts and behavior so that we no longer feel guilty of our sin nor inadequate in God's eyes. We must come to know that we are righteous in God's sight regardless of our behavior and thereby find the peace and the rest that is promised to us in Matthew 11:28,29. We must begin to "renew our minds" as we read in Romans 12:2. It is the inner peace that comes from God's rest that every believer (and every non-believer for that matter) is seeking. When we have peace with God, then our feelings of guilt and anxiety are replaced with God's rest. The Bible describes this as a "peace that passes understanding." The joy that is brought about by an inner peace enables us to be everything that God wants us to be. Inner peace and joy **set us free** from guilt so we can be effective ministers of the gospel for Jesus Christ.

Romans 8:1, 2
1. *There is therefore now no condemnation to them which are in Christ Jesus who walk not after the flesh, but after the spirit.*
2. *For the law of the spirit of life in Christ Jesus has made us free from the law of sin and death.*

God does not condemn us and neither should we condemn ourselves. We only tend to condemn ourselves when we continue to walk in the flesh and not in the spirit as stated in verse 1 above. In scripture, *"walking after the flesh"* is synonymous with striving to do the works required by the law (behavior), and *"walking in the spirit"* is synonymous with believing in God's promises (faith). Walking in the flesh is when a person has more confidence in what he can do for himself than what he believes God can do for him. Those who walk in the flesh apply natural reasoning instead of supernatural reasoning to determine what to do and how to do it. People who walk in the flesh generally feel that they can or must earn their way by doing what the law requires. They feel God will bless them only if they do something first. People who walk in the flesh believe they earn God's favor by "being good."

Conversely, those who walk in the Spirit have confidence in the promises of God and not in their own strength. They don't question the promises of God with human reasoning. They simply act by faith and believe God will do what he says he will do in his word. People who walk in the spirit simply accept the fact that God has justified them because of the sacrifice of Christ and for no other reason. These believers realize that it is God's grace that makes their justification full, not what they do or how they behave.

God wants us to walk in the Spirit, not in the flesh. We are to **walk by faith, not by sight.** That means we are to behave according to what we believe and know from the Word of God. We base our behavior on our understanding of what God has done to redeem us rather than to strive to justify ourselves with God by trying to comply with behavioral laws and guidelines. Again, those will be discussed in the chapter on sanctification. Justification comes first by faith and that leads to sanctification. We must get justification and sanctification in the right order. It is actually the order of things that is so important. Faith must come first. Faith will always lead to good works because good works are a "reasonable" response to the wonderful gift that God has given us. The error is when we get our behavior and our believing out of order. Putting good works first in order to gain favor with God (and why else would we put them first?) will never lead to faith. Because, if we can gain favor with God by our behavior, then Christ's sacrifice on the cross becomes of no use to us as stated in **Galatians 5:4**

4. *Christ is become of no effect unto you, whosoever of you are justified by the law; ye are fallen from grace.*

One of the first things believers must grasp by faith is how God sees us through the redeeming work of Christ. He *"calls those things that are not as though they were!"* **(Romans 4:17)**. We are not righteous in our actual behavior, but God calls us righteous as though we were living perfectly. He doesn't look at us, nor does he treat us according to the way we are now, but according to the way we will ultimately be when the work of Christ is finally perfected in us. And he can do that because Jesus paid the price for our sins and became our righteousness. So God has chosen to see us through the covering blood of Christ. Of course, this only applies to those who have believed in Christ as their savior and confessed him as their Lord.

Romans 4:7 and 8
7. *Blessed are they whose iniquities are forgiven, and whose sins are covered.*
8. *Blessed is the man to whom the Lord will not impute sin.*

Chapter Two

Sanctification

John 17:11-20
11. *And now I am no more in the world, but these are in the world, and I come to thee. Holy Father, keep through thy own name those whom thou hast given to me, that they may be one, as we are.*
12. *While I was with them in the world, I kept them in thy name: those that thou gavest to me I have kept, and none of them is lost, but the son of perdition; that the scripture might be fulfilled.*
13. *And now I come to thee; and these things I speak in the world,* **that they may have my joy fulfilled in themselves.**
14. *I have given to them thy word; and the world hath hated them, because they are not of the world, even as I am not of the world.*
15. *I pray not that thou shouldest take them out of the world, but* **that thou shouldest keep them from the evil.**
16. *They are not of the world, even as I am not of the world.*
17. **Sanctify them through thy truth: thy word is truth.**

18. *As thou hast sent me into the world, even so have I also sent them into the world.*
19. ***And for their sakes I sanctify myself, that they also may be sanctified through the truth.***
20. *Neither pray I for these alone, but for them also who shall believe on me through their word;*

In the previous chapter we discussed **Justification**. In this chapter we're going to learn about **Sanctification**.

We learned that the definition of *Justification* is: to prove or show to be just or right; to qualify; to fit exactly. Let's look at the definition of *Sanctification*:

- the state of growing in divine grace as a result of Christian commitment after baptism or conversion.
- to give moral or social sanction to
- to free from sin

Jesus prayed that the Father would sanctify believers through the truth of His word. Now that we have been deemed Justified - (qualified, just and righteous) through the blood of Jesus and by faith, God wants us to become like Jesus. He wants to change our hearts and our lifestyles. He wants us to quit being like the people of this world who are ruled by the sin nature, and He wants us to strive to become like Him. This work in us is called sanctification. Unlike Justification, which is instantaneous, sanctification is a progressive work that begins with justification and then continues for as long as we live in the earthly body. Sanctification is the progressive change from carnal thinking and behaving to being like Jesus.

1 Thessalonians 4:3,4
3. *For **this is the will of God,** even your sanctification, that ye should abstain from immorality:*
4. *That each one of you should know how to possess his vessel in sanctification and honor*;

Justification, as we learned in the previous chapter, is the result of our faith. We are justified by faith. Sanctification is a process that involves our will. Even though God calls us righteous because of the blood of Jesus, we are not yet practicing a righteous lifestyle. Our hearts are not yet perfected. **We** must **decide** to have a right heart and live a righteous lifestyle. In the two verses above, we are told that "**we** should abstain" and that "**we** should know how" to live a righteous lifestyle. Our sanctification depends on us making the willful decision and then the willful commitment to change how we behave.

2 Timothy 2:19 - 26

19. *Nevertheless, the foundation of God standeth sure having this seal, The Lord knoweth them that are his. And let everyone that nameth the name of the Christ depart from iniquity.*
20. *But in a great house there are not only vessels of gold and of silver, but also of wood and of earth; and some to honor, and some to dishonor.*
21. *If a man therefore purge himself of these, he shall be a fit vessel unto honor, sanctified and meet for the master's use and prepared unto every good work.*
22. *Flee also youthful lusts: but follow righteousness, faith, charity, peace, with them that call on the Lord out of a pure heart.*
23. *But foolish and unlearned questions avoid, knowing that they do gender strifes.*
24. *And the servant of the Lord must not strive; but be gentle unto all men, apt to teach, patient,*
25. *In meekness instructing those that oppose themselves; if God peradventure will give them repentance to the acknowledging of the truth;*
26. *And that they may recover themselves out of the snare of the devil, who are taken captive by him at his will.*

There are three important aspects in this passage of scripture: 1, that God knows them that are His and that they should depart from iniquity; 2, that those who purge themselves become fit for the master's use and will obtain different rewards; and 3, that acknowledging the truth and repentance will recover the believer from the snare of the devil.

The scripture calls for us to depart from iniquity, purge ourselves, flee youthful lusts, follow after righteousness, faith, charity, and peace; avoid foolish and unlearned questions, not to strive, but to be gentle and patient. These are not natural behaviors. They are, however, the objectives that God would have us seek after. They are learned behaviors. They require commitment and dedication. These are decisions that are made only by those who have committed themselves to follow after God. God knows that these are His people because they follow after Him.

Now let's be careful to understand the definition of sanctification. Where the definition says "to grow in divine grace" it is referring to the one who is being sanctified. We grow in grace as we make progress from the carnal man to the image of God. It doesn't mean that we earn more of God's grace. We already have one hundred percent of God's grace the moment we accept Christ. Growing in grace means that we become more like Him. So, the most important point is this: *We are the ones who benefit from the process of sanctification!* Let's look at some scriptures:

Acts 26:18
18. *To open their eyes, and to turn them from darkness to light, and from the power of Satan to God, that they may receive forgiveness of sins, and inheritance among them who are sanctified by faith that is in me.*

God wants to sanctify us for our benefit, rather than for His. Sanctification moves us away from the power of the flesh and the Devil, and closer to the power of God. This is the battlefield for the believer. This is where we find ourselves struggling between the lusts of the flesh and the desire to do what is right in the sight of God. We are drawn to God by the truth and the power of the Holy Spirit on one hand, and we are being tempted by Satan and the lust of the flesh on the other.

Paul deals with this very struggle in great detail in Romans Chapter 7. We want to be pleasing to God, but we find it very hard, if not impossible, to stop doing those things we know are not pleasing to Him. The end result of our sin nature is GUILT, which often leads to _self_-condemnation.

GUILT will have either a positive or a negative affect on us. The degree of guilt is what determines whether the affect will be positive or negative. Only a "normal" degree of guilt will have a positive affect. A "normal" degree of guilt

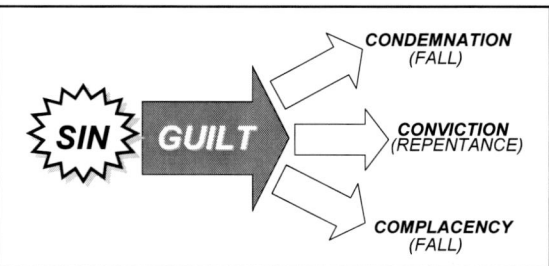

will result in "conviction." Conviction is what the Holy Spirit brings upon us when our thoughts and behavior are not aligning with what God wants for us. The Spirit brings conviction so that we will see the error of our ways and repent. Spiritual conviction is given to us to bring us to a place of repentance whereby we confess our sin and make the commitment to refrain from repeating the undesirable behavior. **1John 1:9** assures us that if we confess our sins, God is faithful and just to forgive us and to cleanse us from all unrighteousness. When we feel cleansed and free from guilt, we then feel comfortable going on with God. If we do not repent and ask God to forgive us, we find it very uncomfortable to go on with God. Keeping unrepented sin makes us feel like hypocrites and makes us tend to shy away from God. We do not like our unrepented sin under the scrutiny of God. In this case the guilt is positive because it causes us to see something undesirable in our life, confess it openly to God and make the change that will bring us closer to what God wants us to be. Now, whether we repent or not does not determine our salvation. Remember, that is absolutely the result of accepting Christ's sacrifice. However, it will affect our reward in heaven as stated in **Acts 26:18** above. Let's clarify that before we look at the negative affects of guilt.

1Corinthians 3:11 – 15

11. *For other foundation can no man lay than that is laid, which is Jesus Christ.*
12. *Now if any man build upon this foundation gold, silver, precious stones, wood, hay, stubble;*
13. *Every man's work shall be made manifest: for the day shall declare it, because it shall be revealed by fire; and the fire shall try every man's work of what sort it is.*
14. *If any man's work abide which he hath built thereupon, he shall receive a reward.*
15. *If any man's work shall be burned, he shall suffer loss: but he himself shall be saved; yet so as by fire.*

Verse 13 talks about every man's work being made manifest. These are the works that we do either for God or for self after we are justified. The works done for God and His cause are like gold, silver, or like precious stones. These works will survive the trial by fire. They will not be consumed by it and they will result in heavenly reward. The works done for self are likened to wood, hay or stubble. As these are tried by fire, it is obvious that they will be burnt up. Those that are burnt up are works motivated by self. Those that remain are works that are done unselfishly for the Kingdom of God. The outcome of the trial by fire will determine the heavenly reward, but not to the point that the person can lose his or her salvation. This is clearly stated in verse 15.

So, even though the nature of works only has an outcome on our heavenly reward, it is important to see that Satan can also use our guilt to destroy us. This is only possible if we allow our guilt to become extreme and something other than the "normal" degree of guilt. There are two degrees of guilt that are not normal: too much guilt and too little guilt.

In the first case, too much guilt, Satan tries to convince us that we are so disobedient that God becomes disappointed or even disgusted with us. Satan can only be successful, if he can **convince us** to quit going on with God by an act of our will. We, **by our own choosing**, condemn ourselves and walk away from God. Satan does not have the power to separate us from God, but we have the power, by our own will, to walk away from God. We know that the devil is a liar, but when we are down on ourselves because of excess guilt, it can be easy to listen to his lies. God loves us unconditionally and the devil knows that. So he waits to strike when we are most vulnerable, in our time of guilt. He uses our time of weakness to convince us to condemn ourselves. Too much guilt leads to self-condemnation.

We must also beware not to write off guilt as meaningless. This usually comes from rationalizing the word of God until we have too little guilt. This is a natural defense mechanism that some might use to counteract too much guilt. This is another way the devil lies to us. He knows that God loves us no matter what, so he attempts to stretch this truth to an extreme degree to make us comfortable thinking we can do as we please. The danger here is that having too little guilt will lead to complacency. We get to a place where we begin to feel so comfortable in our sin, that we disregard God's desire for our sanctification altogether. If we get complacent due to too little guilt, we tend to move away from God. We read the Bible less and we may even stop going to church. In reality, the things of God make us uncomfortable. They make us remember that we are accepting our sin.

As you can see, both extremes lead to a falling away from God. One is self-condemnation due to giving guilt too much power and the other is complacency due to giving guilt too little power.

Both result in us making the conscious decision to move away from God. As long as we are in this body, we will sin. But, by the grace of God, we can confess our sin and be cleansed from all unrighteousness. There are two important aspects of this truth. First, we will sin. Second, we can be cleansed. Let's see how that is possible.

1 Corinthians 1:30
30. *But of him are ye in Christ Jesus, who from God is made to us wisdom, and righteousness, and sanctification, and redemption:*

This verse clearly tells us that Christ is our wisdom, our righteousness, our sanctification and our redemption. It is in Christ, by faith, that we are these things. We believe in Jesus and God imparts to us Christ's character and nature. Even though we continue to sin, God has made a way for our redemption, righteousness and sanctification. That way is Jesus. But if we continue to sin, aren't we falling short of what God wants us to be?

The illustration from the last chapter on justification helps us see that the answer to this question. After we are justified by faith the moment we

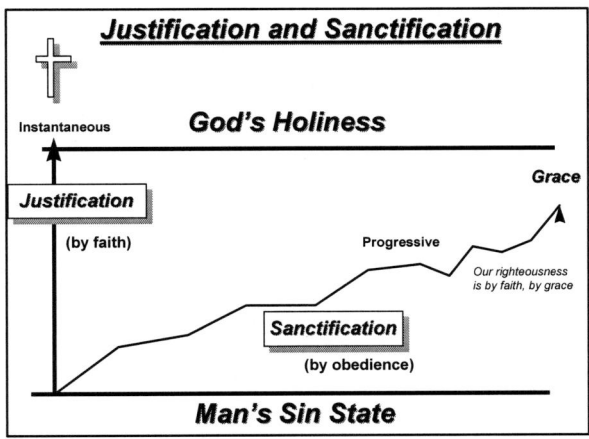

accept Christ, our sanctification begins. The Holy Spirit begins to show us things in our lives that are not appropriate for a child of God. In most new Christians, there are many things that are revealed and dealt with in the first few months after conversion. However, most of us find a few things that are difficult for us to quit. It is a fact that we are not capable of removing every undesirable behavior from our life as long as we occupy this earthly body. We will continue to sin no matter how committed we are to living righteously. This is where the wonderful grace of God makes up the difference. As the illustration shows, we will fall short of God's holiness. Each of us will achieve a different degree of success in our own strength, but we will all fall short of the glory of God. Wherever we are in our walk, God's grace makes up the difference. We are right in His site because of His grace. As stated in 1Corinthians 1:30, Christ is our righteousness and our sanctification.

1 Corinthians 6:11
11. *And such were some of you: but ye are washed,* ***but ye are sanctified,*** *but ye are justified* ***in the name of the Lord Jesus, and by the Spirit of our God.***

If we look at the scripture leading up to this verse, we see that we were all once involved in things of the carnal spirit, but now we are washed in the blood. We are sanctified and justified in the name of Jesus and by the Spirit of God. We must understand that God has already done the work of justification and sanctification in those who believe him. The important thing to remember is that we must continue to press on toward the mark of the high calling in Christ Jesus.

Hebrews 2:11
11. *For both he that sanctifieth and they who are sanctified are all of one: for which cause he is not ashamed to call them brethren,*

We are now part of the family of God. Too often, we hear teaching that God will one day come for a church without spot or wrinkle, implying that the church is not yet without spot or wrinkle. This is ridiculous. The church is already without spot or wrinkle and always has been. This is so because the church is the body of Christ. How can the body of Christ have any spot or wrinkle? The church is not a building; it is a group of people. It is the group of people who follow Christ. Christians are the body of Christ. Therefore, Christians are without spot or wrinkle. Christians are justified and sanctified in Christ. God calls those things that are not as though they were.

Hebrews 10:10

10. *By which will **we are sanctified** through the offering of the body of Jesus Christ once for all.*

The essence of this verse is that our sanctification is eternal through the offering of the body of Jesus Christ by the will of God, the Father. It is God who decided that Christians would be justified and sanctified by Christ. We need simply accept that truth by faith. Again, this is the purpose of this book. God made the promise. He made the way. Are we able to accept the promise and enter into the rest of God by faith?

Hebrews 10:14
14. *For by one offering **he hath perfected forever them that are sanctified.***

Some will argue that we are not truly sanctified until we have rid ourselves from all unrighteousness. But that is not what this verse says at all. It says that **by one offering** He has perfected them that are sanctified. It was the offering of Christ that achieved the perfection in us, not our own labor of good works.

2Corinthians 12:5 - 10
5. *Of such an one will I glory: yet of myself I will not glory, but in mine infirmities.*
6. *For though I would desire to glory, I shall not be a fool; for I will say the truth: but now I forbear, lest any man should think of me above that which he seeth me to be, or that he heareth of me.*
7. *And lest I should be exalted above measure through the abundance of the revelations, there was given to me a thorn in the flesh, the <u>messenger of Satan</u> to buffet me, lest I should be exalted above measure.*
8. *For this thing I besought the Lord thrice, that it might depart from me.*
9. *And he said unto me, <u>My grace is sufficient for thee: for my strength is made perfect in weakness.</u> Most gladly therefore will I rather glory in my infirmities, that the power of Christ may rest upon me.*
10. *Therefore I take pleasure in infirmities, in reproaches, in necessities, in persecutions, in distresses for Christ's sake: for <u>when I am weak, then am I strong.</u>*

This passage is most often taught incorrectly. The infirmity that was given to Paul was not a physical affliction such as an injury or illness. It wasn't a condition of the body tissue. Paul, in verse 5, says that he glories only in his infirmities. If this is the case, then an infirmity wouldn't buffet Paul. It would be a good thing, not a bad thing. But Paul speaks of this "thorn in the flesh" as an undesirable thing. Not something he could glory (be proud of) in. The thorn was given to keep Paul from becoming too proud of the fact that he was being given the abundance of revelations. Now, even though the thorn was brought by a messenger of Satan, we must realize that it was God that sent the messenger. The reasoning behind this is that the thorn was something that was good for Paul because it kept him from becoming "exalted above measure." Knowing what we know about Satan, we should not believe that Satan would do anything that was good for Paul. Satan would love nothing more than for Paul to become exalted above measure, for he that exalteth himself shall be abased and he that humbleth himself shall be exalted.

Another reason we know it was God that sent the thorn is found in verses 8 and 9. Paul prayed three times that the Lord would take the thorn away, but God said that His grace was sufficient, and that God's strength is greatest when we ourselves are weak. Paul found something in this thorn that was weakness to him. Not a physical infirmity because those gave Paul something to glory about. It was something that Paul didn't like in himself. We know from Romans 7:7, *What shall we say then? Is the law sin? God forbid. Nay, I had not known sin, but by the law: for I had not known lust, except the law had said, Thou shalt not covet.* Paul's lust was covetousness. It was covetousness, or some other lust, that was the thorn in Paul's flesh.

We too, have lusts that we cannot seem to overcome.

God wants us to be dependent upon Him. We need a Savior. When we are weak, then He is strong (and we are strong also). If we were able to live righteously in our own strength, then we would not need Christ, and His death on the cross would have been in vain.

So we see another important truth here. That even our sanctification is complete in Jesus' blood. Even though God wants us to abstain from evil and to live righteously, it is not to "make it" in His sight, but rather, it is to benefit us. We will be happier, more fulfilled and full of joy. As such, we can be and will be much more effective for God.

Chapter Three

Righteousness

Matthew 5:20
20. *For I say unto you, That except your **righteousness** shall exceed the **righteousness** of the scribes and Pharisees, ye shall in no case enter into the kingdom of heaven.*

When we see a statement like this, we should make every effort to understand exactly what it means to us. In this case, we must understand what the term "righteousness" means, because entering into heaven depends upon it. Certainly, all of us want to enter into the kingdom of heaven. The truth is, there is a difference of understanding of "righteousness" among Christians. It's one of the reasons there are so many different denominations considering that all use the same Bible.

What is ***righteousness*?**

Philippians 3:9
9. *And be found in him, **not** having mine own righteousness, which is of the law, but (having) that which is through the faith of Christ, the righteousness which is of God **by faith**:*

This scripture tells us that there are two kinds of righteousness:
- my own righteousness which is of the law, and
- righteousness which is of God by faith

Let me suggest by inference, that if the one which is of God is by "faith", then the one that is of the law is by "obedience?" (to the law). Therefore:

My righteousness = of the law = **obedience** to the law = behavior

My righteousness = of God = by **faith** = behavior

Looking at this another way, If my righteousness is of the law, then I must be obedient to the law to be righteous. Therefore, my behavior will focus on being obedient to the law. In this case, I earn my righteousness through my own works of obedience. My righteousness comes as the result of what I do and don't do. My righteousness is of the law.

On the other hand, if my righteous is of God by faith, then I must have faith in God for my righteous. Therefore, my behavior must focus on the fact that God gave me righteous through the work of Christ on the cross, which I accept by exercising my faith. In the latter case, I cannot focus on being obedient to the law or else I risk obtaining my own righteous, which the verse says is of the law. Another way to say that is "self-righteousness."

So one kind of righteousness (my own righteousness) is appropriated by obedience and the other is appropriated by faith. One is earned by works (by doing), those works being a behavior which complies with the do's and don'ts given to man by God whether by the law or by some other means like the teachings of the New Testament scriptures. The other righteousness is not earned at all, but it is accepted by man, through faith (by believing), as a gift from God.

Romans 5:16 -17
16. *And not as it was by one that sinned, so is the **gift**: for the judgment was by one to condemnation, but the **free gift** is of many offences unto justification.*
17. *For if by one man's offense death reigned by one; much more they which receive abundance of grace and of the **gift** of **righteousness** shall reign in life by one, Jesus Christ.*

Righteousness is a gift from God to those who believe. We obtain righteousness by faith, simply accepting the gift, which is from God through Jesus Christ. It is still my righteousness because I am the beneficiary, but it is a gift from God that explains the meaning of the term "righteousness of God." He is my righteousness.

There are many more verses in the Bible teaching us the exact same truth.

Romans 3:21
21. *But now the **righteousness of God** without the law is manifested, being witnessed by the law and the prophets;*
22. *Even the **righteousness of God** which is by faith of Jesus Christ unto all and upon all them **that believe**; for there is no difference:*

Matthew 5:6
6. *Blessed are they which do hunger and thirst after righteousness: for they shall be filled (with the righteousness of God).*

Matthew 6:33
33. *But seek ye **first** the kingdom of God, and **his** righteousness; (by faith) and all these things shall be added unto you.*

Romans 1:17
17. *For therein is the **righteousness of God** revealed from faith to faith: as it is written, **The just shall live by faith**.*

Romans 4:3

3. *For what saith the scripture? Abraham **believed** God, and it was counted unto him for righteousness.*

Romans 4:13
13. *For the promise, that he should be the heir of the world, was not to Abraham, or to his seed, through the law, but through **the righteousness of faith**.*

Romans 4:5-6
5. *But to him that **worketh not**, but believeth on him that **justifieth the ungodly**, his **faith** is counted for righteousness.*
6. *Even as David also describeth the blessedness of the man, unto whom God **imputeth righteousness without works**,*

So let's answer the question of our first point, *"What is righteousness?"*

True righteousness is a gift from God, which we accept by faith that motivates us to a new behavior.

That brings us to another question: *"How does our **righteousness** affect our **behavior**?"*

Romans 6:16
16. *Know ye not, that to whom ye yield yourselves servants to obey, his servants ye are to whom ye obey; whether of sin unto death, or of **obedience unto righteousness**?*

Romans 6:19
19. *I speak after the manner of men because of the infirmity of your flesh: for as ye have yielded your members servants to uncleanness and to iniquity unto iniquity; even so now **yield your members servants to righteousness** unto holiness.*

The scripture certainly exhorts us to be obedient unto righteousness. For example, Jesus said, *"Keep my commandments."* The Bible constantly encourages us to live a clean and holy lifestyle, being loving, honest, caring, and abstaining from sin. So how can we reconcile this call to "good works" with what we just learned about imputed righteousness?

Righteousness that comes from being obedient to the law depends entirely on our ability to comply with the requirements. If we succeed, we feel good about ourselves and we feel God is pleased with us and loves us. However, if we are not successful being obedient, then we feel guilty and that God is disappointed with us and doesn't love us. We become insecure in God and we become afraid. Our behavior becomes focused on complying with the letter of the law so we can feel good about ourselves. As we fall short of absolute holiness, we turn to comparing ourselves with others to see how well we're doing. If we're doing better than most, then we become confident that we are pleasing God and will enter the kingdom of heaven. This behavior is precisely what is referred to as "self-righteousness" (which is of the law). Our righteousness has now become dependent on our works. This is exactly what the religious leaders of Israel did and which is referred to in our key scripture. The righteousness of the scribes and Pharisees was not sufficient for them to be acceptable to God because it was of their own making. This is very clearly stated in:

Rom. 10:1-4
1. *BRETHREN, my heart's desire and prayer to God for Israel is, that they might be saved.*
2. *For I bear them record that they have a zeal of God, but not according to knowledge.*
3. *For they, <u>being ignorant of God's righteousness, and going about to establish their own righteousness, have not submitted themselves unto the righteousness of God.</u>*
4. *For <u>Christ is the **end of the law for righteousness**</u> to every one that **believeth**.*

Striving for righteousness by complying with the law is the wrong behavior. It is exemplified in the story of the Pharisee and the Publican who went to the temple to pray.

Luke 18:10-14
10. *Two men went up into the temple to pray; the one a Pharisee, and the other a publican.*
11. *The Pharisee stood and prayed thus with himself, God, I thank thee, that I am not as other men [are], extortioners, unjust, adulterers, or even as this publican.*

12. *I fast twice in the week, I give tithes of all that I possess.*
13. *And the publican, standing afar off, would not lift up so much as [his] eyes unto heaven, but smote upon his breast, saying, God be merciful to me a sinner.*
14. *I tell you, this man went down to his house justified [rather] than the other: for every one that exalteth himself shall be abased; and he that humbleth himself shall be exalted.*

The Pharisee said he **obeyed** all the law and was glad he was not like the sinner praying next to him. There he was, basing his standing with God on his own works and feeling good about himself because he felt he stacked up pretty well against the Publican, a sinner.

Meanwhile, the Publican was confessing his sinfulness and asking the Lord to forgive him. He acknowledged his need for a savior. He acknowledged his inability to please God with his own works and asked God to make up the difference. Jesus said the Publican went back home justified rather than the Pharisee.

What, then, is the correct righteous behavior?

Romans 8:4
4. *That the righteousness of the law might be fulfilled in us, who walk not after the flesh, but after the Spirit.*

Galatians 2:21
21. *I do not frustrate the grace of God: for if righteousness come by the law, then Christ is dead in vain.*

Once we understand that God has <u>given us righteousness in Jesus Christ</u>, we are <u>motivated to respond</u> with a behavior appropriate for what God has done. We, being exceedingly grateful and thankful, respond by yielding to the leading of the Holy Spirit (walking after the Spirit and not the after the flesh) and not frustrating the grace of God. We <u>renew our minds</u> and endeavor to live our lives according to the direction that God has given us in His Word. Our behavior, our lifestyle, and our works become **products of our faith** motivated by the free gift of righteousness. God went first; we respond with our good works.

Romans 12:1, 2
1. *I beseech you therefore, brethren, by the mercies of God, that ye present your bodies a living sacrifice, holy, acceptable unto God, which is your reasonable service.*
2. *And be not conformed to this world: but be ye transformed by the renewing of your mind, that ye may prove what is that good, and acceptable, and perfect, will of God.*

Holiness is not a rigid requirement; it is a **reasonable response**. It is important for us to understand that whether we respond with good works or not does not affect God's love for us one bit. What it does affect is the reward we will receive at the judgement seat of Christ as stated in **1Corinthians 3**. If God's love were affected by our behavior, then it would be "conditional" love. But we know that His love is "unconditional."

Romans 9:30
30. *What shall we say then? (Answer) That the Gentiles, which followed not after righteousness, have attained to righteousness, even the righteousness which is of faith.*

Romans 10:10
10. *For with the heart man believeth unto righteousness; and with the mouth confession is made unto salvation.*

2Corinthians 5:21
21. *For he hath made him to be sin for us, who knew no sin; that we might be made the righteousness of God in him. (Be made; not become)*

Ephesians 5:9
9. *For the fruit of the Spirit is in all goodness and righteousness and truth*

Philippians 1:11
11. *Being filled with the fruits of righteousness, which are by Jesus Christ, unto the glory and praise of God.*

<u>Righteousness by works</u> **never, never, never** leads to grace (entering into God's rest), but grace (entering into God's rest) **always, always, always** leads to good works.

We can only give grace when we have received grace, and we can only give unconditional love when we have received unconditional love.

Let us not then frustrate the grace of God by continuing to try to earn our own righteousness, nor by continuing to behave like an unknowledgeable sinner. If righteousness can be attained by our own behavior, then Christ died in vain. We could have done it ourselves. But that is not the case.

Chapter Four

The Old Testament and the Law; The New Testament and Sin

Romans 7:1 - 6
1. *Know ye not, brethren, (for I speak to them that know the law,) how that the law hath dominion over a man as long as he liveth?*
2. *For the woman which hath an husband is bound by the law to her husband so long as he liveth; but if the husband be dead, she is loosed from the law of her husband.*
3. *So then if, while her husband liveth, she be married to another man, she shall be called an adulteress: but if her husband be dead, she is free from that law; so that she is no adulteress, though she be married to another man.*
4. *Wherefore, my brethren, ye also are become dead to the law by the body of Christ; that ye should be married to another, even to him who is raised from the dead, that we should bring forth fruit unto God.*
5. *For when we were in the flesh, the motions of sins, which were by the law, did work in our members to bring forth fruit unto death.*

6. *But now we are delivered from the law, that being dead wherein we were held; that we should serve in newness of spirit, and not in the oldness of the letter.*

Given what we've covered up to this point, we get the impression that it is okay to sin. Is it? To answer that question, let's look at the difference between the Old and New Testaments (Covenants).

Paul uses marriage as the metaphor of the two covenants, the Old and the New. While the woman is married, she is bound to her husband and subject to the laws of marriage. If she marries another man while her husband is alive, then she is an adulterer. But, if her husband is dead, then she is free from the former law of marriage and she can marry without becoming an adulterer.

So it is with the Old and New Testaments. Verses 4 and 6 tell us we are dead to the law and delivered from it. Verse 6 says we should **"serve in newness of spirit, and not in the oldness of the letter."** This is important to answering our question, "Is it okay to sin?" and to help us understand what is and isn't sin.

Romans 7:7-14
7. *What shall we say then? Is the law sin? God forbid. Nay, I had not known sin, but by the law: for I had not known lust, except the law had said, Thou shalt not covet.*
8. *But sin, taking occasion by the commandment, wrought in me all manner of concupiscence. For without the law sin was dead.*
9. *For I was alive without the law once: but when the commandment came, sin revived, and I died.*
10. *And the commandment, which was ordained to life, I found to be unto death.*
11. *For sin, taking occasion by the commandment, deceived me, and by it slew me.*
12. *Wherefore the law is holy, and the commandment holy, and just, and good.*
13. *Was then that which is good made death unto me? God forbid. But sin, that it might appear sin, working death in me by that which is good; that sin by the commandment might become exceeding sinful.*

14. *For we know that the law is spiritual: but I am carnal, sold under sin.*

Looking at these verses, Paul examines two important things:
1. The law was good in that it showed Paul the sin that was in him. Verse 8 says that without the law, sin was dead. That means that there was no awareness of the sin nature because there was no standard to reveal it. So the law made the sin nature manifest.
2. Because the law reveals sin, it brings death to the sinner as stated in verses 10 through 13.

Now Paul brings the two together, the Old Testament Law and the deliverance from it through Jesus Christ.

Romans 7:14 – 25

14. *For we know that the law is spiritual: but I am carnal, sold under sin.*
15. *For that which I do I allow not: for what I would, that do I not; but what I hate, that do I.*
16. *If then I do that which I would not, I consent unto the law that it is good.*
17. *Now then it is no more I that do it, but sin that dwelleth in me.*
18. *For I know that in me (that is, in my flesh,) dwelleth no good thing: for to will is present with me; but how to perform that which is good I find not.*
19. *For the good that I would I do not: but the evil which I would not, that I do.*
20. *Now if I do that I would not, it is no more I that do it, but sin that dwelleth in me.*
21. *I find then a law, that, when I would do good, evil is present with me.*
22. *For I delight in the law of God after the inward man:*
23. *But I see another law in my members, warring against the law of my mind, and bringing me into captivity to the law of sin which is in my members.*
24. *O wretched man that I am! who shall deliver me from the body of this death?*
25. *I thank God through Jesus Christ our Lord. So then with the mind I myself serve the law of God; but with the flesh the law of sin.*

Here is the dilemma of the law and sin. Paul says he finds a law, a principle, "that when I would do good, evil is present with me." It is the sin nature in us that makes us want to do what we shouldn't do, and not do the things we should.

The more we try to live righteously and exhibit Christian behavior to others, the more we become aware of just how wretched, how utterly weak and pitiful we are in our flesh. And this causes us to feel guilty and unworthy of God's love. But we can be delivered from that dilemma as Paul was. He stated his deliverance clearly in verses 24 and 25.

"Who shall deliver me from the body of this death? I thank God through Jesus Christ our Lord. *(and here it is!!)* <u>**So then, with the mind, I myself serve the law of God, but with the flesh, the law of sin.**</u>**"**

It is the struggle of the spirit against the flesh. It is the difference between walking in the spirit (serving the law of God with my mind) and walking in the flesh (serving the law of God with my body).

Romans 8:1-8

1. *There is therefore now no condemnation to them which are in Christ Jesus, who walk not after the flesh, but after the Spirit.*
2. *For the law of the Spirit of life in Christ Jesus hath made me free from the law of sin and death.*
3. *For what the law could not do, in that it was weak through the flesh, God sending his own Son in the likeness of sinful flesh, and for sin, condemned sin in the flesh:*
4. *That the righteousness of the law might be fulfilled in us, who walk not after the flesh, but after the Spirit.*
5. *For they that are after the flesh do mind the things of the flesh; but they that are after the Spirit the things of the Spirit.*
6. *For to be carnally minded is death; but to be spiritually minded is life and peace.*
7. *Because the carnal mind is enmity against God: for it is not subject to the law of God, neither indeed can be.*
8. *So then they that are in the flesh cannot please God.*

Here's the bottom line of renewing our minds. No condemnation (verse 1) frees us to be spiritually minded so we can walk after the spirit and not after the flesh, which is pleasing to God. Verses 6, 7 and 8 help summarize several important points. The carnal mind is death. It is enmity against God. It is not subject to the law of God, nor can it become subject to it, so they that are in the flesh cannot please God. No manner of behavior motivated by the carnal mind can earn favor with God. But, to be spiritually minded is life and peace.

We're working toward the answer to our question. "Is it okay to sin?" What was the expectation of the Old Testament? The answer is obedience.

Obedience to what? Answer: The Law.

What is the expectation of the New Testament? The answer is righteous by **faith**. What is righteousness by faith? Answer: To be spiritually minded, living and walking in the Spirit.

So, we're comparing several things here: The Old and New Testaments; The Law and Righteousness; Obedience and faith, and Walking in the Flesh and Walking in the Spirit.

Hebrews 8:6-13 (a better covenant)

6. *But now hath he obtained a more excellent ministry, by how much also he is the mediator of a better covenant, which was established upon better promises.*
7. *For if that first covenant had been faultless, then should no place have been sought for the second.*
8. *For finding fault with them, he saith, Behold, the days come, saith the Lord, when I will make a new covenant with the house of Israel and with the house of Judah:*
9. *Not according to the covenant that I made with their fathers in the day when I took them by the hand to lead them out of the land of Egypt; because they continued not in my covenant, and I regarded them not, saith the Lord.*
10. *For this is the covenant that I will make with the house of Israel after those days, saith the Lord; I will put my laws into their mind, and write them in their hearts: and I will be to them a God, and they shall be to me a people:*

11. *And they shall not teach every man his neighbour, and every man his brother, saying, Know the Lord: for all shall know me, from the least to the greatest.*
12. *For I will be merciful to their unrighteousness, and their sins and their iniquities will I remember no more.*
13. *In that he saith, A new covenant, he hath made the first old. Now that which decayeth and waxeth old is ready to vanish away.*

Jesus came to fulfill the law and bring an end to the first covenant so He could establish a better covenant. The Old Covenant, as explained in verse 9 was one in which God didn't regard the people because they continued not in His covenant. He says the New Covenant is going to be different. The difference is stated in verses 10 and 13.

10. **For this is the covenant that I will make with the house of Israel after those days, saith the Lord; I will put my laws into their <u>mind</u>, and write them in their <u>hearts</u>: and I will be to them a God, and they shall be to me a people:**

13. **In that he saith, A new covenant, he hath made the first old. Now that which decayeth and waxeth old is ready to vanish away.**

There is no longer a list of do's and don'ts given in a written law. Instead, God writes His law in our minds and hearts. This is extremely important when we look at the next chapter about what sin is and what sin is not.

In addition to writing His laws in our minds and hearts, He goes on to say that...

<u>**"I will be merciful to their unrighteousness and their sins and iniquities will I remember no more."**</u>

What can be added to make this statement any more clear?

Hebrews 9:11-14

11. *But Christ being come an high priest of good things to come, by a greater and more perfect tabernacle, not made with hands, that is to say, not of this building;*

12. *Neither by the blood of goats and calves, but by his own blood he entered in once into the holy place, having obtained eternal redemption for us.*
13. *For if the blood of bulls and of goats, and the ashes of an heifer sprinkling the unclean, sanctifieth to the purifying of the flesh:*
14. *How much more shall the blood of Christ, who through the eternal Spirit offered himself without spot to God, purge your conscience from dead works to serve the living God?*

The main point here is that the Old Testament is dead and gone, done away with, and that it has no bearing whatsoever on our relationship with God today. The Old Testament has no jurisdiction over us. It is given to us because it is important for our edification in other ways. It helps us understand God and His principles by showing us the history of God's relationship with Israel and by giving us typological examples of New Testament truth. The one essential thing it does is to lay the foundation for authenticating the New Testament and Jesus as the Christ.

Galatians 4:21 through 5:6

21. *Tell me, ye that desire to be under the law, do ye not hear the law?*
22. *For it is written, that Abraham had two sons, the one by a bondmaid, the other by a freewoman.*
23. *But he who was of the bondwoman was born after the flesh; but he of the freewoman was by promise.*
24. *Which things are an allegory: for these are the two covenants; the one from the mount Sinai, which gendereth to bondage, which is Agar.*
25. *For this Agar is mount Sinai in Arabia, and answereth to Jerusalem which now is, and is in bondage with her children.*
26. *But Jerusalem which is above is free, which is the mother of us all.*
27. *For it is written, Rejoice, thou barren that bearest not; break forth and cry, thou that travailest not: for the desolate hath many more children than she which hath an husband.*
28. *Now we, brethren, as Isaac was, are the children of promise.*

29. *But as then he that was born after the flesh persecuted him [that was born] after the Spirit, even so it is now.*
30. *Nevertheless what saith the scripture? Cast out the bondwoman and her son: for the son of the bondwoman shall not be heir with the son of the freewoman.*
31. *So then, brethren, we are not children of the bondwoman, but of the free.*
1. *Stand fast therefore in the liberty wherewith Christ hath made us free, and be not entangled again with the yoke of bondage.*
2. *Behold, I Paul say unto you, that if ye be circumcised, Christ shall profit you nothing.*
3. *For I testify again to every man that is circumcised, that he is a debtor to do the whole law.*
4. *Christ is become of no effect unto you, whosoever of you are justified by the law; ye are fallen from grace.*
5. *For we through the Spirit wait for the hope of righteousness by faith.*
6. *For in Jesus Christ neither circumcision availeth any thing, nor uncircumcision; but faith which worketh by love.*

Since the Old Testament is gone, we are no longer under the requirement of obeying the Law. In fact, it is <u>disaster</u> for those who try to be obedient to the Law, because verse 4 says those who do are fallen from grace and the sacrifice of Jesus Christ doesn't do them any good.

Since this is true, we must recognize that disobedience to the Old Testament Law is not synonymous with sin described in the New Testament. If the two were the same, then anyone who obeyed the Law would be sinless, which means they would be justified. They would be saved by their own works (called "deeds" in scripture). But the scripture says;

Romans 3:20
20. *Therefore <u>by the deeds of the Law there shall no flesh be justified</u> in His sight: for by the Law is the knowledge of sin.*

Galatians 2:16

16. Knowing that *a man is not justified by the works of the Law*, but by the faith of Jesus Christ, even we have believed in Jesus Christ, that we might be justified by the faith of Christ, and not by the works of the law, for *by the works of the law shall no flesh be justified.*

Galatians 2:21
21. I do not frustrate the grace of God, for *if righteousness come by the law, then Christ is dead in vain.*

So "being good" (obeying the law) was not the Old Testament criteria for acceptance by God. We know that Moses and David committed murder among other sins. Rahab the harlot and the thief on the cross both met the criteria for acceptance by God, and it was not their righteous living.

Obedience to the law was required by the Old Covenant, not for the justification of the person, but to reveal the sin nature in man. That was so the person would recognize his own inadequacies and become totally dependent on God. God wants us to be dependent upon Him, not upon ourselves.

If the Old Testament required obedience to the law, and the Old Testament is done away with, then what does the New Testament require of the child of God? We could say something simple like "not sinning" or "being righteous" but those terms wouldn't give us a clue as to what we would have to do in our daily lives. Besides, **1Cor. 6:12 and Rom. 14:14** tell us that all things are lawful for us. So what is it that God expects from us? Fortunately, the scripture tells us.

Galatians 5:13-26
13. *For, brethren, ye have been called unto liberty; only use not liberty for an occasion to the flesh, but by love serve one another.*
14. *For all the law is fulfilled in one word, even in this; Thou shalt love thy neighbour as thyself.*
15. *But if ye bite and devour one another, take heed that ye be not consumed one of another.*
16. *This I say then, Walk in the Spirit, and ye shall not fulfil the lust of the flesh.*
17. *For the flesh lusteth against the Spirit, and the Spirit against the flesh: and these are contrary the one to the other: so that ye cannot do the things that ye would.*

18. *But if ye be led of the Spirit, ye are not under the law.*
19. *Now the works of the flesh are manifest, which are these; Adultery, fornication, uncleanness, lasciviousness,*
20. *Idolatry, witchcraft, hatred, variance, emulations, wrath, strife, seditions, heresies,*
21. *Envyings, murders, drunkenness, revellings, and such like: of the which I tell you before, as I have also told [you] in time past, that they which do such things shall not inherit the kingdom of God.*
22. *But the fruit of the Spirit is love, joy, peace, longsuffering, gentleness, goodness, faith,*
23. *Meekness, temperance: against such there is no law.*
24. *And they that are Christ's have crucified the flesh with the affections and lusts.*
25. *If we live in the Spirit, let us also walk in the Spirit.*
26. *Let us not be desirous of vain glory, provoking one another, envying one another.*

All throughout New Testament scripture we're <u>invited</u> and <u>exhorted</u> to "yield our members and present our bodies," to God and to "walk in the spirit." And even though Paul gives us a list of visible "works of the flesh," the New Testament doesn't give us an explicit list of do's and don'ts like the Old Testament. God said that under the New Covenant, He would write His laws in our minds and in our hearts **(Hebrews 8:10).** God has given us the Holy Spirit to guide us into his truth and righteous living. It is the fruit of the Spirit described in verses 22 and 23 above that become our goals for living.

Here are some scriptures that <u>exhort</u> us to live righteously.

Romans 6:13
13. *Neither <u>yield</u> ye your members as instruments of unrighteousness unto sin: but <u>yield</u> yourselves unto God, as those that are alive from the dead, and your members as instruments of righteousness unto God.*

1Corinthians 15:34
34. *<u>Awake</u> to righteousness, and sin not; for some have not the knowledge of God: I speak this to your shame.*

Romans 12:1-2

1. *I beseech you therefore, brethren, by the mercies of God, that ye present you bodies a living sacrifice, holy, acceptable unto God, which is your reasonable service.*
2. *And be not conformed to this world, but be ye transformed by the renewing of your mind, that ye may prove what is that good, and acceptable, and perfect will of God.*

Here, I want to reiterate the point that holiness is a reasonable response, not a rigid requirement. We should live righteously, rather than we must live righteously. That mind set helps us be obedient to the laws that God has written in our mind and hearts.

So, we know that God wants us to exhibit righteous behavior, but just what kind of behavior is that? What does righteous behavior look like?

The answer is given in the "fruit of the Spirit" listed in **Galatians 5**, and in the Sermon on the Mount in **Matthew chapters 5 through 7**, beginning with the beatitudes. These scriptures explain the difference between the "letter" and the "spirit" of the law. **(Romans 7:6)**.

Righteousness in the New Testament is an attitude, an allegiance, and a goal. It is a matter of the heart and a pursuit that we press on toward. It's the prize, the mark of the high calling. It has something to do with behavior, but it's more than behavior alone. It is a determination and an allegiance to God and His ways. It must be rooted in the heart.

It's also more than just the heart alone too, as James explains, "show me your faith without works, and I'll show you my faith by my works." James also says, "faith without works is dead." It would be the same to have millions of dollars, but then not ever use it for anything. I remember a saying, "There must be a root for there to be fruit, but the fruit is the proof of the root." This saying relates to this teaching in this way; "there must be faith for there to be works, but the works are the proof of the faith." How can there be faith and no works as a result of that faith? The works are the "reasonable response."

The "Fruit of the Spirit" are all of those things. They are attitudes, goals and behaviors. To manifest the Fruit of the Spirit, one must "walk in the Spirit" and "live in the Spirit."

So, even though we have liberty, and have been set free, and have been made righteous by the blood of Christ, we are still called, exhorted, beseeched and every way encouraged to live for God and not to ourselves. It is a choice that we make. It's an attitude that leans us toward the things of God. It's an allegiance to God and to His kingdom. It's a goal that we set our eyes upon and pursue by faith and works. But the faith is the foundation and must come first. And then the works, the result of the faith and built upon it. Faith is the solid rock foundation (Christ) and works is the house built upon that foundation. If the house is built without the foundation, then it is built on sinking sand and will certainly fall when the storm beats upon it.

Let's summarize and bring it all into balance so far. First, God has redeemed us from the curse of the law and has given us liberty from our own sinfulness. Our sins are no longer judged by God.

Romans 5:13
13. *For until the law, sin was in the world: but sin is not imputed when there is no law.*

Romans 5:20
20. *Moreover the law entered, that the offense might abound. But where sin abounded, grace did much more abound.*

Romans 6:14
14. *For sin shall not have dominion over you: for ye are not under the law, but under grace.*

Hebrews 8:12
12. *For I will be merciful to their unrighteousness and their sins and their iniquities will I remember no more.*

Second, we are free to behave in any manner we so please. It is okay to sin. (Egads!! Did I say that?) It is okay from the standpoint that God (and we ourselves) know that we will continue to sin as long as we are in this mortal body and in this world. Sin is a fact of life as long as we are on earth. If it wasn't okay to sin, we'd all be doomed already. But "if we confess our sin, He is faithful and just to forgive us our sins, and to cleanse us from all unrighteousness." **(1John 1:9)**

Since I know this flies in the face of everything you've been taught through sermons and Sunday School, I'd better divert here and explain the point more clearly.

Acts 11:1-18.

1. *And the apostles and brethren that were in Judaea heard that the Gentiles had also received the word of God.*
2. *And when Peter was come up to Jerusalem, they that were of the circumcision contended with him,*
3. *Saying, Thou wentest in to men uncircumcised, and didst eat with them.*
4. *But Peter rehearsed the matter from the beginning, and expounded it by order unto them, saying,*
5. *I was in the city of Joppa praying: and in a trance I saw a vision, A certain vessel descend, as it had been a great sheet, let down from heaven by four corners; and it came even to me:*
6. *Upon the which when I had fastened mine eyes, I considered, and saw fourfooted beasts of the earth, and wild beasts, and creeping things, and fowls of the air.*
7. *And I heard a voice saying unto me, Arise, Peter; slay and eat.*
8. *But I said, Not so, Lord: for nothing common or unclean hath at any time entered into my mouth.*
9. *But the voice answered me again from heaven, What God hath cleansed, that call not thou common.*
10. *And this was done three times: and all were drawn up again into heaven.*
11. *And, behold, immediately there were three men already come unto the house where I was, sent from Caesarea unto me.*
12. *And the Spirit bade me go with them, nothing doubting. Moreover these six brethren accompanied me, and we entered into the man's house:*
13. *And he shewed us how he had seen an angel in his house, which stood and said unto him, Send men to Joppa, and call for Simon, whose surname is Peter;*
14. *Who shall tell thee words, whereby thou and all thy house shall be saved.*
15. *And as I began to speak, the Holy Ghost fell on them, as on us at the beginning.*

16. Then remembered I the word of the Lord, how that he said, John indeed baptized with water; but ye shall be baptized with the Holy Ghost.
17. Forasmuch then as God gave them the like gift as [he did] unto us, who believed on the Lord Jesus Christ; what was I, that I could withstand God?
18. When they heard these things, they held their peace, and glorified God, saying, Then hath God also to the Gentiles granted repentance unto life.

Peter was taught all his life that there were common and unclean things that he was forbidden to eat. Every sermon and Sunday School lesson Peter had ever heard told him this, and so did the scriptures. But GOD, was introducing a New Covenant, a covenant of grace that extended His blessing to the gentiles, the common people. Peter (and those who were with him) had a very difficult time accepting this change in their theology. The Lord had to give Peter the vision three times and remind him of His new promises about the Holy Spirit before Peter finally "renewed his mind." I use this to make an analogy to the statement I just made, that it is okay to sin. You're having just as much trouble believing that right now as Peter had when God first gave him the vision of the unclean things. Don't get hung up on that just yet because I'm going to clarify it as we continue.

Third, we are exhorted (and called) by the scriptures to live righteously before God. Fourth, living righteously without sin under the New Covenant means having an attitude and an allegiance to God and making the fruit of the Spirit our goals for personal living.

Romans 6:1
1. What shall we say then? Shall we continue in sin, that grace may abound? **God forbid.**

Romans 6:15
15. What then? Shall we sin, because we are not under the law, but under grace? **God forbid.**

Galatians 2:17
17. But if, while we seek to be justified by Christ, we ourselves also are found sinners, is therefore Christ the minister of sin? **God forbid.**

Galatians 2:16-21
16. *Knowing that a man is not justified by the works of the law, but by the faith of Jesus Christ, even we have believed in Jesus Christ, that we might be justified by the faith of Christ, and not by the works of the law: for by the works of the law shall no flesh be justified.*
17. *But if, while we seek to be justified by Christ, we ourselves also are found sinners, is therefore Christ the minister of sin? God forbid.*
18. *For if I build again the things which I destroyed, I make myself a transgressor.*
19. *For I through the law am dead to the law, that I might live unto God.*
20. *I am crucified with Christ: nevertheless I live; yet not I, but Christ liveth in me: and the life which I now live in the flesh I live by the faith of the Son of God, who loved me, and gave himself for me.*
21. *I do not frustrate the grace of God: for if righteousness come by the law, then Christ is dead in vain.*

These scriptures clearly summarize two points: walking in the spirit, not in the flesh, and that we are no longer under the law. The term "God forbid" should be understood as saying, "absolutely not." The first two scriptures from Romans 6 say, that just because we are free from the law that it does not give us an excuse to sin. Galatians 2:17 says that, even though we are justified righteous by Christ, and we continue to sin, does that make Christ the minister of sin? And the emphatic answer is "absolutely not." Christ is not the minister of sin, he is the coverer of sin. We will continue to sin. It is in us to do so. It is the sin nature that comes in the mortal flesh that we occupy. But we have one who covers the sin, one who forgives us our sins, and one who cleanses us from all unrighteousness, if only we believe.

Chapter Five

What Is Sin?

Romans 6:1 - 6
1. *What shall we say then? Shall we continue in sin, that grace may abound?*
2. *God forbid. How shall we that are dead to sin, live any longer therein?*
3. *Know ye not, that so many of us as were baptized into Jesus Christ were baptized into his death?*
4. *Therefore we are buried with him by baptism into death: that like as Christ was raised up from the dead by the glory of the Father, even so we also should walk in newness of life.*
5. *For if we have been planted together in the likeness of his death, we shall be also in the likeness of his resurrection:*
6. *Knowing this, that our old man is crucified with [him], that the body of sin might be destroyed, that henceforth we should not serve sin.*

There is no doubt in my mind that **sin** and **grace** are among the most difficult subjects we encounter as we study the word of God. Most of the Book of Romans deals with the subject of **sin** and **grace**. This teaching is absolutely necessary as the follow-up to **justification** and **sanctification** and that's exactly why Paul is writing what he is here in Romans chapters 5, 6, 7 and 8. It takes Paul four full chapters and parts of several other chapters just to cover the many aspects associated with *sin* and *grace.*

Let's begin by asking the question, "WHAT IS SIN?"

Romans 14:23
23. *And he that doubteth is condemned if he eateth, because he eateth not from faith:* ***for whatever is not from faith is sin.***

James 4:17
17. *Therefore, to him **that knoweth to do good, and doeth it not**, to him it is sin.*

1 John 5:17
17. ***All unrighteousness is sin:*** *and there is a sin not unto death.*

These are the only three scriptures in the New Testament that <u>define</u> sin. They tell us what sin is. From them, we can absolutely conclude that there are two broad categories of sin.

The first category of sin includes: **ALL UNRIGHTEOUSNESS.** This category includes all of the acts of a person that are **harmful** or **hurtful** to God or to another person. Without exception, these acts (behavior) are committed because of **selfishness in the heart** of the person committing the act.

All unrighteousness is what is covered by The Ten Commandments:
- no other Gods
- no graven images
- taking God's name in vain
- keeping the sabbath holy
- honoring father and mother
- killing
- adultery
- stealing
- bearing false witness
- coveting

The second category of sin includes: **ACTS WITHOUT FAITH.** This category includes all acts of a person which are done to obtain a sense of self-righteousness by creating a man-made set of

do's and don'ts that are not in the first category. This category contains both **Romans 14:23 and James 4:17**, so it includes the sins of omission. Sins which would fall into this category are:
- Doing anything <u>you believe</u> is sin
- Not doing something good <u>you believe</u> you should do.

We usually have no problem understanding the first category. These are *absolute*. God commanded them and we all are obligated to obey them. The important thing to understand about the Ten Commandments is that they **cover all unrighteousness (all the harmful and hurtful things that a person can do against God or another person.)**

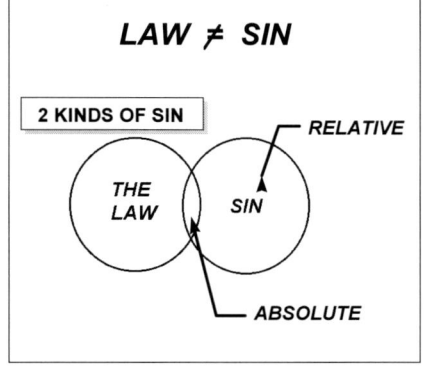

The second category is the one we have all the trouble with. It contains many <u>disputable</u> things because what is sin to one person is not the same for another person. I refer to these as Relative sin.

Romans 14:1-3
1. *Him that is weak in the faith receive ye, but not to doubtful disputations.*
2. *For one believeth that he may eat all things: another, who is weak, eateth herbs.*
3. *Let not him that eateth despise him that eateth not; and let not him which eateth not judge him that eateth: for God hath received him.*

Paul introduces things he calls ***doubtful disputations.*** As we read through this chapter, we recognize that the term refers to things contained in the Old Testament law. The first example he uses is eating meats or not. The second, in verse 6, is regarding one day above another. He uses these as examples to teach the conclusion expressed in Romans 14:14, ***"there is nothing unclean of itself, <u>but to him that esteems it unclean, to him it is unclean.</u>"***

This is an important distinction because it teaches us that some sin is relative. Relative sin is dependent upon what a person esteems (considers important), and no two of us esteem the same things alike. We each have our own unique viewpoints as to what is important and what is not.

Romans 14:22-23
22. *Hast thou faith? have it to thyself before God. Happy is he that condemneth not himself in that thing which he alloweth.*
23. *And he that doubteth is damned if he eat, because he eateth not of faith: for whatsoever is not of faith is sin.*

These two verses clearly state the essence of sin, which is not of faith. Happy is he that condemns not himself in the things that he allows. Notice that it is the person who condemns himself of the things he allows. For example, if I eat meat and it doesn't feel right to me, then I condemn myself for eating it. There is nothing wrong with eating meat. It is just that when I feel it is wrong and I do it anyway, then I feel guilty and I condemn myself. On the other hand, if I do not feel that there is anything wrong with eating meat, I can eat it without any guilt whatsoever. Then I am happy because I do not condemn myself for the thing that I do. With this truth in mind, let's look at some scriptures that speak about "being freed from sin."

So, sin is one of two things: it is not abiding by the Ten Commandments, or it is doing or not doing anything that is not of faith.

Romans 6:7
7. *For he that is dead is **freed** from sin. {freed: Gr. **justified**}*

Now that we know what sin is, we need to know how to be freed from it. We need to know how to get out from under the control of sin and its effects on us. This is the main theme of chapters 6, 7 and 8 of Romans, so let's begin in chapter 6.

We learned that we are justified by faith, that we are sanctified by faith and that we are no longer held accountable for our deeds as long as we walk with the Lord, as long as we confess our sins, He is faithful and just to forgive us. This is God's GRACE! Paul spent a lot of time in chapters 3, 4 and 5 proclaiming this truth. But now, he has to caution the people not to go to the other extreme.

So he begins chapter 6 as he does! *"Shall we continue in sin that grace may abound? **God forbid!**"*

To briefly summarize this chapter, Paul shows us that we sin because we are tempted to do the things that are forbidden to us. If we're told we can't do something, then we have an increased desire to do that. That tendency is called the ***Sin Nature***. The law contained many things like this, things that tempted us to do what we shouldn't. It is this desire that puts us into bondage to sin. But remember I said earlier that it was never intended that man should obey the law. **The law was given for another reason.**

Romans 5:20, 21
20. *Moreover **the law entered, that the offence might abound**. But where sin abounded, grace did much more abound:*
21. *That as sin hath reigned to death, even so might grace reign through righteousness to eternal life by Jesus Christ our Lord.*

Romans 3:20
20. *Therefore by the deeds of the law there shall no flesh be justified in his sight: **for by the law is the knowledge of sin.***

These scriptures help us to see that the law was ***not*** given with the intention that we might obey it unto righteousness, but that the law would make us aware of sin, and that sin might abound! The law was given to make us aware that we have a Sin Nature, and that we need a savior. It was to show us that our flesh rises up against laws that forbid us to do something.

Romans 6:4-14
4. *Therefore we are buried with him by baptism into death: that like as Christ was raised up from the dead by the glory of the Father, even so we also should walk in newness of life.*
5. *For if we have been planted together in the likeness of his death, we shall be also in the likeness of his resurrection:*
6. *Knowing this, that our old man is crucified with him, that the body of sin might be destroyed, that henceforth we should not serve sin.*

7. *For he that is dead is freed from sin.*
8. *Now if we be dead with Christ, we believe that we shall also live with him:*
9. *Knowing that Christ being raised from the dead dieth no more; death hath no more dominion over him.*
10. *For in that he died, he died unto sin once: but in that he liveth, he liveth unto God.*
11. *Likewise reckon ye also yourselves to be dead indeed unto sin, but alive unto God through Jesus Christ our Lord.*
12. *Let not sin therefore reign in your mortal body, that ye should obey it in the lusts thereof.*
13. *Neither yield ye your members as instruments of unrighteousness unto sin: but yield yourselves unto God, as those that are alive from the dead, and your members as instruments of righteousness unto God.*
14. *For sin shall not have dominion over you: for ye are not under the law, but under grace.*

In these verses, Paul encourages us by telling us that we are already dead to sin, and then tells us **to reckon ourselves dead to sin** (verse 11). But I want to focus on what is said here in verses 12,13 and 14 because they are the main point of this chapter.

verse 12: You don't have to let your lust rise up any more, because there is no longer anything unlawful to tempt you
verse 13: Because you don't have to worry about breaking any laws, you can now be free to serve God without guilt
verse 14: Sin can no longer tempt you because there is no longer any law, same as verse 12, nothing is unlawful.

Romans 6:14
14. *For sin shall **not** have dominion over you: **for ye are not under the law, but under grace.***

Now combine **Romans 6:14 with Romans 5:13!**

Romans 5:13
13. (For until the law sin was in the world: ***but sin is not imputed when there is no law.***

But it's Romans 5:13 that is of utmost importance to us now! We are no longer under the law, therefore sin is not imputed

to us! This is why we can say that sin no longer has dominion over us.

Before we go on to the next part, let's look at **John 8:1-11**
1. *Jesus went unto the mount of Olives.*
2. *And early in the morning he came again into the temple, and all the people came unto him; and he sat down, and taught them.*
3. *And the scribes and Pharisees brought unto him a woman taken in adultery; and when they had set her in the midst,*
4. *They say unto him, Master, this woman was taken in adultery, in the very act.*
5. *Now Moses in the law commanded us, that such should be stoned: but what sayest thou?*
6. *This they said, tempting him, that they might have to accuse him. But Jesus stooped down, and with his finger wrote on the ground, as though he heard them not.*
7. *So when they continued asking him, he lifted up himself, and said unto them, He that is without sin among you, let him first cast a stone at her.*
8. *And again he stooped down, and wrote on the ground.*
9. *And they which heard it, being convicted by their own conscience, went out one by one, beginning at the eldest, even unto the last: and Jesus was left alone, and the woman standing in the midst.*
10. *When Jesus had lifted up himself, and saw none but the woman, he said unto her, Woman, where are those thine accusers? hath no man condemned thee?*
11. *She said, No man, Lord. And Jesus said unto her, Neither do I condemn thee: go, and sin no more.*

Jesus does not condemn the woman accused of adultery, one of the Ten Commandments (absolute sin.) Now this is such a wonderful revelation, that Paul immediately has to throw out the yellow (red) flag.

15. *What then? shall we sin, because we are not under the law, but under grace? By no means.*

Again, our human nature is to go to the other extreme. So Paul goes on to explain that we are to serve God with a pure heart. If

we just go on sinning because it is not imputed to us, then we continue to serve sin, and not God. We still have a choice. **Let's choose God because of His wonderful grace, not sin because of His wonderful grace.**
	We serve God because we want to, because we know that it is right. (or as my Pastor used to say, "I don't <u>have</u> to serve God, I <u>get</u> to.") Serving God is best for God and best for us. Only when we serve God can we have the "joy unspeakable" and "peace that passes understanding" that we are all looking for. Anyone who serves God because he HAS TO, is not serving God, but themselves. Only those serving God because they WANT TO are really serving God.

Romans 7:7-9
7. *What shall we say then? Is the law sin? By no means. Nay, I had not known sin, but by the law: for I had not known lust, except the law had said, Thou shalt not covet.*
8. *But sin, taking occasion by the commandment, wrought in me all manner of lust. For apart from the law sin was dead.*
9. *For I was alive apart from the law once: but when the commandment came, sin revived, and I died.*

Chapter Six

Expediency

1 Corinthians 6:12-20

12. *All things are lawful to me, but all things are not expedient: all things are lawful for me, but I will not be brought under the power of any.*
13. *Foods for the body, and the body for foods: but God shall destroy both it and them. Now the body is not for immorality, but for the Lord; and the Lord for the body.*
14. *And God hath both raised up the Lord, and will also raise up us by his own power.*
15. *Know ye not that your bodies are the members of Christ?* **shall I then take the members of Christ, and make them the members of an harlot? By no means**.
16. *What? know ye not that he who is joined to an harlot is one body? for two, saith he, shall be one flesh.*
17. *But he that is joined to the Lord is one spirit.*
18. **Flee immorality.** *Every sin that a man doeth is outside the body; but he that committeth immorality sinneth against his own body.*
19. *What? know ye not that* **your body is the temple of the Holy Spirit** *which is in you, which ye have from God, and* **ye are not your own?**

20. *For **ye are bought with a price**: therefore glorify God in your body, and in your spirit, which are God's.*

What shall we say then? Shall we continue in sin that grace may abound? God forbid!

As we've been looking at this scripture, we needed to define what sin is, so we could <u>not</u> continue in sin. We found that there are two kinds of sin; those in the Ten Commandments (absolute sin) and those that we, as individuals, consider sin (relative sin). We also discovered that we are no longer under the law. And because of these truths, we are told by the scripture that we are ***dead to and freed from sin***. This freedom from sin, or more accurately stated, this freedom from the ***control and guilt*** of sin, gives us a ***liberty*** that is wonderful and new. Now Paul addresses this new liberty we find for ourselves. He starts with this statement:

*All things are lawful to me, **but** all things are <u>not</u> expedient: all things are lawful for me, **but** I will <u>not</u> be brought under the power of any.*

Let's look first at Webster's definition of "expedient" - "suitable for achieving a specific end", "advisable", or "profitable." So, let's read the scripture with the definition of expedient inserted, *"All things are lawful to me, but all things are not suitable for achieving a specific end." "All things are lawful to me, but all things are not advisable or profitable."* It may be easier to understand this if we relate to something in the natural world. For example, it is not unlawful for you to smoke and drink alcohol, but it is not good for you or for others around you. Smoking and drinking alcohol are not expedient.

There are at least three good reasons not to yield to sin:
First:
We are the body of Christ, the light of the world and the temple of the Holy Ghost. These are good reasons for us to abstain from things that would not be seen by others as "Christian" attitude or behavior. Our mission is to win souls for Christ, and we cannot do that if we offer only the same things the world offers.

1 Corinthians 10:33
33. *Even as I please all men in all things, not seeking my own profit, but the profit of many, that they may be saved.*

People are not seeking after evil and unrighteousness, even though it might appear that they are. The world is seeking after joy and peace. You and I know that these things can only be found in Jesus. We need to show them the way. We need to be examples, good examples that offer the lost and dying world an alternative. Therefore, we should live our lives according to the principles of God. And just in case there is still doubt as to what the principles of God are, they are: *love, joy, peace, long suffering, gentleness, goodness, faith, meekness and temperance.* The Bible says, against these things, there is no law. That means, these are the behaviors we want to learn and use in our daily lives. These are the New Testament "commandments" of God for Christian living.

Second:
There's another reason for living according to these principles. We need to care for the needs and feelings of the others in the body of Christ.
Romans 14:13
13. *Let us **not** therefore **judge one another** any more: but judge this rather, that no man put a **stumbling block or an occasion to fall** in his brother's way.*
1 Corinthians 8:9
9. *But take heed lest by any means this liberty of yours should become a stumbling block to them that are weak.*

Christians regard certain things differently. Some people think certain things are sin while others do not. The Word clearly tells us that different people have different kinds of sin (relative sin). In several scriptures, these differences are referred to as strength and weakness. It is because of these differences that we can have relationship problems between Christians. In one instance, the stronger Christian may put a stumbling block or an occasion to fall in his brother's way. In another instance, the weaker Christian will judge the stronger Christian. Let's look at these two possible relationships.

Romans 15:1
1. *We then that are **strong** ought to bear the infirmities of the **weak**, and not to please ourselves.*

Interestingly enough, strength is related to liberty (liberalism), while weakness is related to obedience (legalism). As Christians, we will find ourselves on one side or the other in every relationship with another Christian, because no two of us see things exactly the same. Therefore, there will be times when you feel at liberty to do something that the other Christian has a problem with. In this case, you are the strong (at liberty) Christian. In another relationship, the viewpoint may be the opposite. In this case you would be the weaker (not at liberty) Christian. Since there will always be these differences, we must learn how to behave or treat the other person in each situation.

As the Strong Christian:
Romans 14:13
13. *Let us not therefore judge one another any more: but judge this rather, that no man put a stumblingblock or an occasion to fall in [his] brother's way.*
Romans 15:1
1. *We then that are strong ought to bear the infirmities of the weak, and not to please ourselves.*

These two verses teach us this. As the strong Christian, when you feel at liberty to do something that is considered by another Christian as sin, then you should not do it in the presence of that person because it will cause grief, discomfort or discouragement of some kind to the other person (a stumbling block). It is easier for the stronger person to adjust to the weaker, and therefore, should do so. Let me phrase that another way. It is easier for the liberal Christian to abstain from something than it is for the obedient Christian to accept it. "We that are strong ought to bear the infirmities of the weak and not to please ourselves." (Romans 15:1)

As the Weak Christian:
Romans 14:3-4
3. *Let not him that eateth despise him that eateth not; and let not him which eateth not judge him that eateth; for God hath received him.*
4. *Who art thou that judgest another man's servant? To his own master he standeth or falleth. Yea, he shall be holden up, for God is able to make him stand.*

Romans 14:13 and 14:3-4 teach us this. As the weaker Christian, when you feel what the other Christian is doing is wrong, your tendency is to judge that person. You might say something like this, "Can you believe what that person is doing? And he calls himself a Christian." These scriptures warn against judging another. They also tell us that when it comes to disputable things (Romans 14:1), or relative sin, what another Christian does is none of our business (Romans 14:4). Look at the following scriptures as they relate to judging one another:

Matthew 7:1-5
1. *Judge not, that ye be not judged.*
2. *For with what judgment ye judge, ye shall be judged: and with what measure ye mete, it shall be measured to you again.*
3. *And why beholdest thou the mote that is in thy brother's eye, but considerest not the beam that is in thine own eye?*
4. *Or how wilt thou say to thy brother, Let me pull out the mote out of thine eye; and, behold, a beam is in thine own eye?*
5. *Thou hypocrite, first cast out the beam out of thine own eye; and then shalt thou see clearly to cast out the mote out of thy brother's eye.*

Luke 6:37
37. *Judge not, and ye shall not be judged: condemn not, and ye shall not be condemned: forgive, and ye shall be forgiven:*

Romans 2:1
1. *Therefore thou art inexcusable, O man, whosoever thou art that judgest: for wherein thou judgest another, thou condemnest thyself; for thou that judgest doest the same things.*

Psalms 18:25
25. *With the merciful thou wilt shew thyself merciful; with an upright man thou wilt shew thyself upright;*

James 2:13
13. *For he shall have judgment without mercy, that hath shewed no mercy; and mercy rejoiceth against judgment.*

Our conflict is with spiritual wickedness in high places, not with each other. The devil would like nothing more than to have the body of Christ fighting with itself. Love is the motivation for everything a Christian does.

1 Corinthians 13:1-3
1. *Though I speak with the tongues of men and of angels, and have not charity, I am become as sounding brass, or a tinkling cymbal.*
2. *And though I have the gift of prophecy, and understand all mysteries, and all knowledge; and though I have all faith, so that I could remove mountains, and have not charity, I am nothing.*
3. *And though I bestow all my goods to feed [the poor], and though I give my body to be burned, and have not charity, it profiteth me nothing.*

Notice in these three verses that the "Christian behavior" is <u>nothing</u> if it isn't motivated by love.

Galatians 5:13
13. *For, brethren, ye have been called to liberty; only use not liberty for an occasion to the flesh, but <u>by love</u> serve one another.*

1 Corinthians 10:23
23. *All things are lawful for me, but all things are not expedient: all things are lawful for me, but all things edify not.*
24. *Let no man seek his own, but every man another's good.*

Third:

Finally, a casual attitude to unrighteous living can lead even the strongest believer to destruction. There is a danger in using the liberty we have been given unwisely and selfishly.

1 Peter 2:16
16. *As free, and not using your liberty for a **cloak of maliciousness**, but as the servants of God.*

1 Corinthians 9:27
27. *But I keep under my body, and bring it into subjection: lest by any means, when I have preached to others, I myself should be a **castaway**.*

We cannot have a cloak of maliciousness and still practice the fruit of the Spirit. Let's not focus on the fact that we are freed from sin so we can do unrighteous things, but let's use it rather to help us be free from guilt and condemnation so we can focus on the fruit of the Spirit and live according to the principles of God.

Paul suggests in **1 Corinthians 9:27** that it is possible to be cast away. He would not say this if it were not possible, so we must heed the urging or warning, if you will, to bring our bodies under subjection. The subjection is to the principles of God.

Yes, we are freed from the control and guilt that the knowledge of sin brings on us. All things are lawful to us. But let us use our liberty only to bring glory to God, to build up and edify the church and to love one another.

Romans 12:1-3, 9 - 10 and 21.
1. *I beseech you therefore, brethren, by the mercies of God, that ye present your bodies a living sacrifice, holy, acceptable unto God, which is your reasonable service.*
2. *And be not conformed to this world: but be ye transformed by the renewing of your mind, that ye may*

    prove what is that good, and acceptable, and perfect, will of God.
3. *For I say, through the grace given unto me, to every man that is among you, not to think of himself more highly than he ought to think; but to think soberly, according as God hath dealt to every man the measure of faith.*
9. *Let love be without dissimulation. Abhor that which is evil; cleave to that which is good.*
10. *Be kindly affectioned one to another with brotherly love; in honour preferring one another;*
21. *Be not overcome of evil, but overcome evil with good.*

Chapter Seven

Peace

Luke 2:8-14
8. *And there were in the same country shepherds abiding in the field, keeping watch over their flock by night.*
9. *And, lo, the angel of the Lord came upon them, and the glory of the Lord shone round about them: and they were sore afraid.*
10. *And the angel said unto them, Fear not: for, behold, I bring you good tidings of great joy, which shall be to all people.*
11. *For unto you is born this day in the city of David a Saviour, which is Christ the Lord.*
12. *And this [shall be] a sign unto you; Ye shall find the babe wrapped in swaddling clothes, lying in a manger.*
13. *And suddenly there was with the angel a multitude of the heavenly host praising God, and saying,*
14. *Glory to God in the highest, and on earth peace, good will toward men.*

The announcement by the angelic host in this "Christmas" scripture was never meant to imply that mankind would live in harmony without war and other disputes. In fact, Jesus said in **Luke 12:51, *"Suppose ye that I am come to bring peace on earth? I tell you Nay; but rather division."*** The peace spoken of by the angels referred to a different kind of peace—the peace of God, and the good will of God toward them that believed. It is a Godly peace, not a worldly peace.

1. peace with God (reconciliation)
2. peace within our spirits (rest)

John 14:27
27. *Peace I leave with you, my peace I give to you: not as the world giveth, give I to you. Let not your heart be troubled, neither let it be afraid.*

In fact, the peace that is spoken of here is a "gift" from God so we could have the peace that passes understanding, in the midst of the storm, in the midst of an evil world in the last days. We need not be afraid.

Jesus says His peace is a different kind of peace. It's not like peace that the world can give, which is only superficial and temporary at best. But He gives true peace. His peace goes to the very depth of our being and it is lasting. It is a supernatural, spiritual peace that transcends reason and understanding. So He comforts us with these words, "let not your heart be troubled, neither let it be afraid." Isn't this what we all want?

So we see then that there are only two places we can be. We can be in God's rest with the peace of God, or we can be outside of His rest with all the troubles and fears that go with it. *Therefore, we must conclude that if we are troubled— filled with anxiety and fear— then we are not where we should be.* (NOTE: By troubled, I'm talking about being troubled in our spirits, having fear, anxiety, stress, depression and so forth.)

"In the world we will have tribulation", that's a different kind of trouble, but Jesus goes on to say, "be of good cheer", and that's the rest I'm talking about. Good cheer in the midst of tribulation.

When Jesus came, he set us free from the law and ordinances so we might have peace, not so we could go out and live recklessly and unrighteously. We are set free from the law and ordinances and in its place we are given the gift of peace with God, and peace within ourselves. God wants you to have His peace in spite of all the trials and temptations (including the weakness of the flesh) that this life will bring.

John 16:33

33. These things I have spoken to you, that <u>in me</u> ye may have peace. In the world ye shall have tribulation: but be of good cheer; I have overcome the world.

The Lord knew we would face many trials and temptations in the world. He knew we were going to face spiritual enemies, and He made provision for us to be strong and to be at peace in the midst of it all. He also knew that if we were going to need peace in the midst of the turmoil, He would need to give us that blessed assurance that we are His, saved, loved and empowered to stand against the wiles of the devil. No Christian would be able to stand if continuously faced with the fear that God, as well as the enemy, was watching for the first sin or transgression that would cause the Christian to lose his salvation and be cast into hell with the unbelievers.

<u>God knew we needed to have peace with Him if we were to be victorious.</u>

Romans 5:1
1. *Therefore being <u>justified</u> **by faith, we have peace with God** through our Lord Jesus Christ:*

Philippians 4:7
7. *And the peace of God, which passeth all understanding, shall **<u>keep</u>** <u>your hearts and minds</u> through Christ Jesus.*

So therefore, we who believe have been given the gift of peace with God, by faith, through the blood of Jesus Christ. God chose to give us this peace in Christ who is the Head and the pre-eminence of all things.

Colossians 1:20
20. *And, having made peace through the blood of his cross, by him to <u>reconcile all things</u> to himself; by him, I say, whether they are things on earth, or things in heaven.*

God gave us this gift, and all He asks is that we accept it, by faith. I will show you that this acceptance by faith is what the scripture refers to as "walking in the Spirit." It's the act of depending on **what God has done**. I will show you that <u>not</u> accepting this gift by faith is what the scripture refers to as "walking in the flesh." This is the act of depending on *what we do ourselves*. This "new understanding" is the essence of the teaching in Romans chapter 8. Paul spends this entire chapter assuring us that we are free from the law, that we are **justified** by God through faith, that God loves us who believe and that nothing can separate us from His love. God does not want us to fear Him from the standpoint that He is watching us closely so He can send us to hell for the things that we do or don't do. That kind of thinking is again, "walking according to the flesh."

We who are freed from the law are now set free to concentrate on loving one another, and not worrying about the weaknesses of the flesh.

Galatians 5:16 says "Walk in the Spirit, and you will NOT fulfill the lust of the flesh."

This gets us back to the struggles we have with guilt, fear, doubt and jealously. When we worry about what the flesh is doing, it comes into conflict with the Spirit. Do I believe that I am justified by grace, or don't I? If I believe it, then I can stop trying to *become* righteous, because I am *already* righteous.

Look at **Galatians 5:17 and 18** together. We're told that the flesh and the Spirit are contrary, that they lust against each other "<u>so that ye cannot do the things that ye would, BUT, IF ye be led of the Spirit, YE ARE NOT UNDER THE LAW.</u>"

What, exactly, does this mean? It means if you are led of the Spirit, you will love thy neighbor as thyself, putting the interests and well-being of others above yourself, not despising or judging one another about the things that you (or they) do. The flesh will continue to lust against the Spirit, and vice versa, but you will CHOOSE to be led of the Spirit and be free from the bondage of sin, **or** you will CHOOSE to be led by the flesh, in which case you will be under the law for your justification. And the scripture says that no flesh shall be justified by the law. And that truth is stated in

Romans 8:6

> 6. *For to be carnally minded is death; but to be spiritually minded is life and peace.*

And that brings us back to the truth of this first point:

John 16:33

> 33. *These things I have spoken to you, that <u>in me</u> ye may have peace. In the world ye shall have tribulation: but be of good cheer; I have overcome the world.*

We <u>can</u> have peace with God, we <u>can</u> have that peace that passes understanding in the midst of trials and tribulation, and we <u>can</u> love one another in spite of our many differences.

Romans 14:17

17. *For the kingdom of God is not food and drink; but righteousness, and peace, and joy in the Holy Spirit.*

Galatians 5:22

22. *But the fruit of the Spirit is love, joy, peace, longsuffering, gentleness, goodness, faith, meekness and temperance.*

Chapter Eight

Glorious Church Without Spot or Wrinkle
"The Body of Christ"

Colossians 1:12-19
12. Giving thanks unto the Father, which hath <u>made us meet to be partakers of the inheritance</u> of the saints in light:
13. Who hath <u>delivered us from the power of darkness</u>, and hath <u>translated us into the kingdom of his dear Son</u>:
14. In whom <u>we have redemption</u> through his blood, <u>even the forgiveness of sins</u>:
15. Who is the image of the invisible God, the firstborn of every creature:
16. For by him were all things created, that are in heaven, and that are in earth, visible and invisible, whether they be thrones, or dominions, or principalities, or powers: all things were created by him, and for him:
17. And he is before all things, and by him all things consist.
18. And <u>he is the head of the body, the church</u>: who is the beginning, the firstborn from the dead; <u>that in all things he might have the preeminence</u>.
19. <u>For it pleased the Father that in him should all fullness dwell</u>;

Eph.5:25-30
25. Husbands, love your wives, even <u>as Christ also loved the church</u>, and gave himself for it;
26. That he might sanctify and cleanse it with the washing of water by the word,
27. That <u>he might present it to himself a glorious church, not having spot, or wrinkle, or any such thing; but that it should be holy and without blemish.</u>
28. So ought men to love their wives as their own bodies. He that loveth his wife loveth himself.
29. For no man ever yet hated his own flesh; <u>but nourisheth and cherisheth it, even as the Lord the church:</u>
30. <u>For we are members of his body, of his flesh, and of his bones.</u>

Our scripture from Colossians tells us some pretty wonderful things that God has already done for those of his creation who confess him as Father.
- he has made us fit to be partakers of the inheritance
- he has delivered us from the power of darkness
- he has translated us into the kingdom of his dear son
- we have redemption, even the forgiveness of sins

All of these things have one profound meaning; they made it possible for us to be the body of Christ, the church. Only by the things that God himself has done, could we become the body of Christ while we yet dwell upon this earth and in these corrupt bodies of our own.

So we are the body of Christ. He made us to be members of His body when we believed on him. He did some spiritual translation and changing that we cannot yet fully comprehend, but he did it. We don't have to understand it; we only have to believe it.

Now, let's summarize the jewels out of the Ephesians scripture reference.
- Christ loved the church and gave himself for it (he loves his own body)
- Christ nourishes and cherishes his body
- We're not only members of his body, but we are members of his flesh and his bones (that's not an exaggeration, that's a reality which I'll try to show you.)

2Corinthians 5:17-18
17. *Therefore if any man be in Christ, he is a new creature: old things are passed away; behold, all things are become new.*
18. *And all things are of God, who hath reconciled us to himself by Jesus Christ, and hath given to us the ministry of reconciliation;*

I'm sure many of you belong to, or have at one time belonged to, a social or professional organization. You almost certainly joined because the organization represented interests that you shared in some way. At first, it would be easy to think that becoming a Christian is much the same. It couldn't be farther from the truth. There is no comparison, and the reason why is revealed in verse 18; "All things are of God."

The first big change is that you are a new creation. You have a new life, quickened by the Holy Spirit and under the jurisdiction of God. While the leadership of an organization might have some influence on you, believe me, it can't hold a candle to the influence of the Holy Ghost and the creator of the universe! **1Corinthians 15:22** says, **"For as in Adam all die, even so in Christ shall all be made alive."** We have been delivered from the curse of sin and death inherited in Adam and have been translated into the kingdom of his dear son, Jesus Christ.

Secondly, we now have a relationship with God, the Father.

So, you're a new creation, all things are new, and all things are of God. You're the body of Christ, the church. Christ is the head, and he loves, nourishes and cherishes his body. That body is us my brothers and sisters!

Now we know that the body and the church are one, and that Christ loves us.

Our scripture also says that Jesus Christ loved the church and gave himself for it, that He might sanctify it and present to himself holy and without blemish.

I'm sure you, like me, have heard preachers and Sunday School teachers refer to the "glorious church without spot or wrinkle." Unfortunately, in some of those messages, the speaker implies that Christ is waiting for the church to become spotless so he can return. They imply that the church has some sort of spot or wrinkle, which of course would be sin. This is a wrong message. It's wrong for two very important reasons; 1) It's wrong to imply that there is sin in the very body of Christ, and 2) even if there could be sin in the body of Christ, it would be wrong to imply that the body itself, (the church), had the ability to rid itself of that sin. Both of these ideas are simply ludicrous. The one and only atonement for the sins of man is, and ever will be, the blood of Jesus Christ, our savior. If Christ were not going to return until the church cleaned up its own act, He would never return. The church without Christ is dead. The body cannot exist without the head.

The songwriter had his theology right when he wrote, "'Tis a glorious church without spot or wrinkle, washed in the blood of the lamb." The body of Christ, the church, is already without spot and wrinkle because it is washed in the blood. Christ gave himself for it to sanctify it, to make it holy so he could present it to himself a glorious church without spot or wrinkle. His body has no blemish, neither can it have blemish. There can be no sin in the body of Jesus Christ. He is the spotless lamb. And we are the beneficiaries, because God the Father wanted it that way.

Ephesians. 1:3-7
3. *Blessed be the God and Father of our Lord Jesus Christ, who hath blessed us with all spiritual blessings in heavenly places in Christ:*
4. *According as he hath chosen us in him before the foundation of the world, that we should be holy and without blame before him in love:*
5. *Having predestinated us unto the adoption of children by Jesus Christ to himself, according to the good pleasure of his will,*
6. *To the praise of the glory of his grace, wherein he hath made us accepted in the beloved.*
7. *In whom we have redemption through his blood, the forgiveness of sins, according to the riches of his grace*

Jesus is the head of the body and the foundation of the church. But we know this only by faith. When Jesus asked Peter to tell him who he believed him to be, Peter said, "Thou art the Son of the Living God." Peter could only say this by faith. And Peter's faith was so great that Jesus said, on this rock (on Peter's faith alone) he would build his church.

We are the church, the body of Christ. Does that mean that we are without spot or wrinkle or any such thing? You better believe it does. We are pure spiritually, made that way by the blood of the Lamb.

Romans 4:17

17. *(As it is written, I have made thee a father of many nations,) before him whom he believed, even God, who quickeneth the dead, and calleth those things which be not as though they were.*

We are a chosen generation, a royal priesthood, a holy nation, a peculiar people. We are unique among the people on the earth. We have been made holy by the blood of Jesus, and He has made us a jewel in the kingdom of God.

Chapter Nine

Entering Into God's Rest

We Have Peace With God

Romans 5:1
1. *Therefore being justified by faith, we have peace with God through our Lord Jesus Christ.*

Peace with God is the first **essential** to entering into God's rest. If we don't have peace with God, we will be in a constant struggle with our flesh (sin nature). It will consume all of our energy which will hinder our ability to be witnesses because it will either cause discouragement or it will make us feel like hypocrites. Discouragement will show and will tend to make the unsaved not want what we have. If we feel like hypocrites, the Devil will badger us about our deception until he can persuade us to give up on ourselves and walk away from God.

Through the teaching of the scriptures, we now know that our faith in the sacrifice Jesus made on the cross justifies us with God. We can rest in the blessed assurance that we are saved and God loves us, unconditionally. We need no longer worry about whether God is pleased with us regardless of our behavior. He is pleased because we have believed and accepted his forgiveness by faith. It is finished.

We Have Peace With Ourselves
John 14:27
27. *Peace I leave with you, **my peace I give to you**: not as the world giveth, give I to you. Let not your heart be troubled, neither let it be afraid.*

Once we have peace with God, we must have peace with ourselves. Once we are convinced that God has forgiven us, we must now forgive ourselves. But peace within ourselves can only come once we have peace with God. God does not want us to be afraid that our sin nature will defeat us. He is able to keep you from falling. Fear is of the devil.

Romans 8:1, 2
1. *There is therefore now <u>no condemnation</u> to them which are in Christ Jesus who walk not after the flesh (works), but after the spirit (faith).*
2. *For the law of the spirit of life in Christ Jesus has made us free from the law of sin and death.*

Walking after the spirit means walking by faith. When we walk by faith, the scripture says that there is no condemnation. God does not condemn us for our behavior. With this truth, we can now have peace with ourselves, even though we are still subject to the sin nature. Because of our acceptance of Jesus and his atoning work by faith, God does not condemn us for our weakness. Since God doesn't condemn us, we must not condemn ourselves. This transformation requires a renewing of the mind. Only Satan will try to persuade you to condemn yourself by telling you are unworthy in God's eyes and that God no longer loves you. Satan is a liar and the father of lies. God loves you. Accept that peace within yourself.

We Have Peace With Others
Galatians 5:13
13. *For, brethren, ye have been called to liberty; only use not liberty for an occasion to the flesh, but <u>by love serve one another</u>.*

1Corinthians 10:23, 24

23. *All things are lawful for me, but all things are not expedient: all things are lawful for me, but all things edify not.*
24. *Let no man seek his own, but every man another's good.*

Once we are free from the guilt of our own sinfulness giving us peace with God and with ourselves, then we are free to focus our energy on loving and serving one another. Jesus said the two greatest commandments are these, "to love God and to love your neighbor as yourself. On these two commandments hang all the law." We are one body, let us serve God as one. We are called to good works. Faith without works is living a lie, and is inconsistent with reason. Serving God and others brings true joy unspeakable and full of glory and a peace that passes understanding.

There remains a rest for God's people. Let us not come short of it because of an evil heart of unbelief. (Hebrews 3 and 4)

The very foundation for entering into God's rest requires that you first accept God's grace.